BUS

S

DO NOT REMOVE
CARDS FROM POCKET

SAFE TRAVEL IN BEAR COUNTRY

Gary Brown

LYONS & BURFORD, PUBLISHERS

*Across the North American
continent are thousands of individuals who,
while working for various agencies and
organizations, in the past and present, have
faithfully, diligently, and repeatedly provided
safety information to travelers in bear
country. To all of you, this book is
gratefully dedicated.*

Copyright ©1996 by Gary Brown

Printed in the United States of America

Illustration on pp. 90-91 by Manuel F. Cheo

Design and composition by Marcy Kass

10 9 8 7 6 5 4 3 2 1

Library of Congress Cataloging-in-Publication Data

Brown, Gary
    Safe travel in bear country / Gary Brown.
        p. cm.
    Includes bibliographical references and index.
    ISBN 1-55821-349-X
    1. Bear attacks—North America—Prevention. 2. Outdoor recreation—North America—Safety measures. 3. Black bear—Behavior. 4. Grizzly bear—Behavior. I. Title.
QL737.C27B77 1995   95-40200
599.74'446—dc20   CIP.

CONTENTS

INTRODUCTION   1

1 THE BEARS — A NATURAL HISTORY   7

The Bear
Bear Habitat
Bear Behavior and Activities
How Bears Think
Bear Sign
Encounters with Humans
Differences Between Black and Grizzly Bears

2 BEAR ATTACKS   33

Provoked Encounters
Unprovoked Encounters
Causes of Encounters/Attacks
A Bear Attack

3 AVOIDING BEAR ENCOUNTERS (ATTACKS)   45

Before You Leave Home—Planning
Arrival in Bear Country
Travel in Bear Country
Other Activites in Bear Country
Women in Bear Country

**4   ENCOUNTERS WITH BEARS
(YOUR ACTIONS AND REACTIONS)**   121

Bear Observed in the Distance—<u>Not</u> Aware of You

Bear Observed in the Distance—Aware of You

A Sow with Cubs

A Bold Black Bear

The Close Encounter—A Confrontation

The Bear Attack

Climbing a Tree to Escape a Bear

Bear Repellents

In Case of Injury

Reporting Observations, Encounters, and Attacks

5   SOME REMINDERS — A SUMMARY   139

6   RECOMMENDED READING   142

INDEX   144

Introduction

How would you react to someone you did not know or recognize, and even perceived as an enemy, entering your yard or home—perhaps surprising you in your kitchen, at the dinner table, or in bed? Wouldn't there be fear, curiosity, uncertainty, and possibly flight or aggression? Maybe you would even describe your potential reactions as unpredictable. I know I might react defensively and so would most anyone. Well, bears react in the same manner. When you enter bear country, you are entering their backyard, their home.

Bear country, or bear habitat, is the area where bears are most likely to be found; where they live; the environment where they find food, shelter, protection, reproductive opportunities, seclusion, and space to be free. And this is, for the most part, scenic vacationland (parks, forests, mountains, undeveloped lands, seashores) where people visit to relax and enjoy a variety of activities, leaving behind the stresses of everyday life.

1

Humans and bears have competed for the same habitat for more than fifty thousand years. During the last two hundred years, expanding human development and activities in North America have resulted in an increasing risk of encounters between bears and people.

To me, bears have long represented something special—majestic, dangerous—an element of wonder and excitement in the forests and meadows. And, after being a park ranger and manager involved for more than thirty years with the interrelationships between people, bears, and bear habitat, my interests and sentiments have not diminished in the least. Besides working in bear country over these years, my overall lifetime interests have taken me into black and grizzly bear country throughout the western United States (including Alaska) and Canada, and the Appalachians of Tennessee and North Carolina. While camping, jogging, dogsledding, hiking, canoeing, kayaking, skiing, and horseback riding, I have observed bears. Some of my encounters with bears have been the result of my failure to take precautions, and others seem to have been the result of a bear's curiosity.

In Denali National Park, while attempting to photograph a bull moose, I imprudently found myself facing a large grizzly bear. I had been silently moving along a wildlife trail in dense brush on a very windy day, and stepped to the edge of a sunlit opening in the vegetation—within twenty feet of the bear. It *was* large. The bright sun shone directly into the bear's eyes as it sniffed, held its head low, staring into the alder thicket where I had by now realized my mistakes (making no noise, being downwind, and encroaching into the bear's space), and was rapidly deciding my next move. Though unable to see into the dark thicket, it had detected something and was attempting to identify the intrusion. I silently backed away, having decided not to talk until the bear moved toward me or made some threatening movement with its head or paws. Soon I was out of sight of the bear, and shortly thereafter reached my vehicle a half mile away from where I could observe the animal grazing on a slope above the alder thicket. Fortunately, it had not charged or followed me.

Bears are curious, usually in their search for food, and that was probably what attracted another large grizzly bear as my wife and I kayaked along the Kobuk River in northwestern Alaska. The bear ran out of dense brush and across the gravel shoreline directly toward us, then turned downstream, closely paralleling the kayak. It encroached into the shallow water, moving closer to us as we frantically paddled. Finally, when we managed to increase the distance between us, the bear stopped and stood on its hind legs, swinging its head from side to side inquisitively, attempting to identify that large blue-and-gray object with the flailing creatures on top.

When you enter bear country you most often do so on the bears' terms, and there is a *risk*. To many people, that risk is a valuable part of using wild country, but everyone must recognize the risk, accept it, and be responsible for their actions. Bears are wild, unpredictable, and dangerous animals, and the prevention of encounters is the key to safe travel in bear country. That is what the following pages are about—avoiding encounters, and thus avoiding disastrous attacks.

This book is designed for both new and experienced users of black bear or grizzly bear country, whether on the highways or trails, whether traveling through or staying overnight in lodges, cabins, motels, hotels, or front or backcountry campsites. It focuses on recreational use, not commercial outfitting, tours, or guided activities—though the information it provides would be of considerable value to outfitters and their clients.

The term "encounter" is used to describe most any type of contact with a bear, including observations. "Attack" is used to refer to a true aggressive charge by a bear, whether or not there is physical contact with a person.

Described are the causes of encounters, the measures recommended to avoid or minimize the potential for conflict, and, finally, how to deal with an attack should it occur. Advice and suggestions are based on the experiences of many bear country travelers and bear authorities. The suggested measures are designed not only to minimize the danger of a bear encounter but to prevent one in the first place. This book contains specific suggestions, but before traveling in bear country, be sure to check with local managing agencies, which may provide even more precise variations.

The information refers to the "normal," most common, type of bear habitat and behavior. Variations occur in individual bears and populations. You should understand that the information is intended to prepare you for as many eventualities as possible but may not address every unpredictable situation that might come up when you use bear country. I strongly believe that nearly all the encounters that have occurred could have been avoided, and that all future ones can be prevented.

Carefully read the book in its entirety as part of your trip planning, even if you acquire it after you leave home and are near your destination. Treat it as a "handbook": in your hand, available, frequently referred to at home, in your motel room or cabin, at the trailhead, at stops along the trail, in camp, and when evaluating your trip and planning your next adventure. Refer to the specific segments that apply to your location and activity—use the book as a checklist. You should understand and remember its information in advance, however, because at the moment of an encounter you will not have the luxury of time to read. The information in this book has enabled thousands of people in North America to safely travel through bear country. Now you can too.

1

The Bears— A Natural History

THE BEAR

Nearly everyone is familiar with a bear of some type: the black bear of North America, the mysterious polar bear of the Arctic, the controversial grizzly bear, the intriguing giant panda of China, or Winnie the Pooh, Yogi, and the forever lovable Teddy Bear.

However, much of your familiarity with wild bears is likely to be "armchair," and not come from being a participant in bear country—a visitor in the realm of bears. Three species of these marvelous mammals exist in North America—the American black bear; the brown bear, including the grizzly bear; and the polar bear.

This book focuses on the American black bear *(Ursus americanus)* and the grizzly bear *(Ursus arctos horribilis)* of Canada and the United States.

As you travel in bear country, a basic understanding and knowledge of these symbols of wildness is an essential foundation for *safe* travel.

7

Black Bear
(Courtesy Yellowstone National Park)

•

Bears are the only large omnivores—meaning that in addition to being big, they generally eat anything and everything. They all have basically the same shape, with heavily constructed, strong, and durable bodies, and they possess enormous strength and power, as displayed by their excellent digging prowess, great speed, and incredible ability to remove walls from buildings or kill (grizzly bear) and carry away an adult elk.

Their curved, strong claws are hard, and may be used to strike prey, rip and tear, or rapidly dig a hole adequate in size to house a bear. However, these impressive implements can also be used with remarkable dexterity

Grizzly Bear
(Courtesy Yellowstone National Park)

to handle foods, retrieve backpacks, and open door latches. (See illustration on page 10.)

A bear's teeth are set in jaws powered by massive muscles, and are designed to bite, shear, hold, grind, and crush.

Though these large wild animals seem to move with a lackadaisical, shuffling gait, giving them the illusion of being slow and clumsy, they actually move with a splendid rhythm and precision. Bears are amazingly swift, attaining speeds of 25 to 40 mph, and are capable of outrunning Olympic sprinters. Although they can maintain their top speed only for short distances, their endurance is exceptional. They have been known to run without a break for ten miles, and they run both uphill

BLACK BEAR

GRIZZLY BEAR

A Comparison of Black and Grizzly Bear Claws

and downhill with speed and agility. Essentially, bears are capable of running 50 percent faster than you! The danger and futility of running from a bear is discussed in chapter four.

Bears are capable of standing unaided on their hind legs. They stand upright to observe or increase sight distance, to fight, to reach foods or prey, or to "mark" (or "sign"). They are capable of walking bipedally, though usually for only a few steps.

•

The bears' senses of *vision*, *hearing*, and *smell* range from good to excellent. People used to believe that their vision was poor. Recent scientific investigations, though, have shown their sight to possibly equal that of humans. They are nearsighted but recognize form and movement at relatively long distances, and their peripheral, color, and night vision are quite reliable.

A bear's sense of hearing is more sensitive than a human's. They have been known to respond to the sound of a camera shutter at more than fifty yards, and to detect normal level human conversation in excess of one-quarter mile.

However, a bear's nose is its key to its surroundings. No animal has a more acute sense of smell. This olfactory sense allows it to avoid humans, and to locate mates and food sources. A bear has been known to detect a human scent more than fourteen hours after the person passed along a trail. Also, a bear has been observed traveling upwind for more than three miles in a direct line to a deer carcass.

The average weight of black bears is 250 pounds (and ranges from 125 to 600 pounds). The black bears of eastern North America are consistently larger than those of the western states, provinces, and territories. Black bears live an average of eighteen years. Grizzly bears average 490 pounds (and range from 350 to 700 pounds), and have an average life span of twenty-five years.

The physical qualities of bears can be summarized as strength, agility, and speed. No animal of equal size is as powerful. Its physical and mental abilities continue to astonish bear experts. The combination of the bear's power, high intelligence, acute awareness of its habitat, and finely tuned, instinctive reactions make it one dangerous wild animal.

BEAR HABITAT

BEAR HABITAT is "bear country," where a bear normally spends its life, year after year, in an environment that meet its requirements for survival.

These requirements are specialized both among black bear and grizzly bear species, and among individuals within each species. Although food is the greatest necessity for all bears, other elements are also essential. They include cover, protection, solitude (enough space not to feel threatened), mating opportunities, and resting and denning sites. "Bear country" may overlap human enclaves such as ranches, lodges, homes, towns, corner service stations, visitor centers, campgrounds, cabins, or other developments.

Black bears may be found in deciduous as well as coniferous forests, in mixed forests, and in swamps, while grizzly bears inhabit mixed forests, areas that are treeless or scarcely forested, and arctic/alpine tundra. These are primary habitats, though both species may also often be observed elsewhere as they travel through their ranges.

Within its habitat an individual remains at the same general elevation, but may range between elevations during day-to-day or week-to-week searches for food. It may also range between elevations seasonally, depending on food sources, and it normally moves to a different elevation to den. Black bears and grizzly bears on the North American continent are generally found between sea level and ten thousand feet, though there are a few isolated exceptions.

The densities of bear populations vary seasonally throughout habitats, with food availability—streams congested with spawning fish, areas of minimal food—being a significant influence. Densities are also influenced by human populations and activities, because bears are displaced by the encroachment of human development and subsequent conflicts. Often, when unable to adapt to these encroachments, bears are crowded into the remaining undeveloped and small habitat areas, which are typically inadequate for their survival.

Bears have home ranges, but are not territorial. They do not defend a territory from other bears. The ranges of adult males (black bear, 42.8 square miles; grizzly bear, 23 to 870 square miles) are normally larger than those of females. Bears move in response to food availability, and the more inadequate a bear's habitat in regard to food, the larger its range will be. Habitat quality also influences bears' sizes. Poor habitats usually produce relatively smaller bears, while an environment with an abundance of food with high nutritional value—such as an area with major fish populations—produces larger bears. Ranges may increase during the fall as food becomes scarce and bears attempt to build fat for hibernation.

BEAR BEHAVIOR AND ACTIVITIES

Feeding

Though they are omnivorous, black and grizzly bears mostly eat vegetation. They appear to have preferences and seasonal needs, though most of what they eat is controlled by the availability of nutritious food sources in their habitat. They must move in response to these sources, seeking food as wandering and opportunistic feeders.

They are generalists, scavengers, and diverse gluttons, and they have large bodies that assist them in surviving long periods of food shortage and poor-quality diets.

Diet varies with the seasons, and bears seldom feed for very long in a single small area. They dig for roots, bulbs, and rodents, sometimes expending an inordinate amount of energy for such small rewards. They graze in meadows, eat berries and fruits, fish along streams, consume new growth shoots in treetops, and scavenge

COMMON BEAR FOODS ARE

roots, frogs, fish, ants, insects,
small vertebrates, rodents, birds, hoofed animals,
crayfish, grubs, carcasses, bees, eggs, human
garbage, berries, mushrooms, grasses, fruits, nuts,
seeds, sedges, honey (including bees), herbs,
acorns, and squirrels.

the carcasses of other animals. Moths and other insects are located beneath rocks and in logs, deftly retrieved with paws and claws, lips and tongue. Bears remember rewarding sources of natural foods, or in some cases human foods and garbage.

They drink water several times a day. The quantity depends on an individual's activities.

Travel

Bears spend their days roving from one location to another, seeking food, searching for a mate, moving to and from a day bed, avoiding people, playing, investigating, and performing countless other activities not understood by humans. They move silently, and either walk or run to reach their destinations.

The routes bears travel vary based on topography and purpose. Some routes serve a specific mission, leading to a predetermined destination, while others are the result of exploration. Bears are capable of negotiating most any terrain, including the most dense vegetation, extremely steep ridges and cliffs, and deep, strong currents of streams.

Most commonly bears travel the routes of least resistance, while avoiding open areas. *This often means the use of trails and other human developments.* Their travel routes might include: bases of cliffs, forest edges, previously established bear trails, other animal trails, hillsides (that have rock ledges to walk on), meadows, ridges, human-constructed trails, roads, developed areas (areas associated with structures, parking areas, campgrounds), shorelines (of streams, lakes, ponds), small passes between hills, saddles, snowfields, and stream bottoms. You could summarize these routes as "just about anywhere"— *and* as areas where humans might also find the easiest and most convenient traveling.

Distance appears to be of no concern to bears, as they are quite capable of traveling more than a hundred miles in a day.

Swimming

Bears' activities are not all terrestrial. In general, they use bodies of water—streams, lakes, and ponds—for pleasure and purpose, and are excellent swimmers. Water must sometimes be traversed during their travels, but quite often it provides a means to escape from insects, cool off,

Grizzly Bears in Stream
(Courtesy Yellowstone National Park)

feed (fish, frogs, crayfish, bugs), relieve itching, hide their tracks, play (wade, sit and splash, soak, float), and swim.

Climbing

Climbing is also important to many bears. They climb trees to feed, to rest, to play, or for safety. Young grizzly and black bears climb naturally; they don't need to learn.

Adult black bears are outstanding climbers, climbing regularly and easily to feed, escape enemies, or, in some areas, hibernate. Their climbing ability declines with age, so older adults climb infrequently for food.

Adult grizzly bears are poor climbers, *not nonclimbers* due to their body weight and claw structure (long and straight, compared to the shorter, hooked claws of black bears). However, adult grizzly bears are readily capable of laddering up trees with low branches and have ascended many feet when necessary.

Play

We humans appear to be most attracted to bears because they play. We especially enjoy the humorous antics of cubs, as well as the humanlike play activities of adult bears. However, this play is more than just the idle activity or recreation that we might interpret it to be. It contributes to the preparation for survival. Play is actually "play fighting," an extremely important course in a young bear's education—one that helps develop social attitudes and physical coordination.

Day Beds

The active life of bears takes its toll and occasionally they need to nap. Located near food sources and often with a commanding view, day beds are used by all bears for short- or long-period resting, and a bear may have several such sites throughout its range. An American black bear will sleep stretched out on the limbs of a tree, in grassy areas, on the ground, or on a bed of conifer needles. A grizzly bear will sleep in forested (or sometimes open) areas, on the ground, on grassy beds, on conifer needles, or in shallow depressions (lined or unlined) dug in the soil or snow.

Reproduction

Reproduction is similar among black and grizzly bears, though some small variations do exist. American black bear females may have their first litter at three to five years of age; grizzly bear sows, at five years. Males of both species become sexually mature earlier than their boldness allows them to compete and participate.

Courtship and mating periods vary between and within each species, depending on habitat and climate. Generally, black bears court and mate during a two- to three-week period in June and July, while grizzly bears are sexually active during a seven- to eight-week period from late May to mid-July. Males may travel great distances to locate a mate. Courting activities are quite noisy, capable of being heard from some distance.

Though mating generally occurs during the spring/ summer, implantation of the fertilized ovum on the uterine wall is delayed until a more appropriate time for the female. Due to this delay the overall gestation period, conception to birth, for both species, is 235 days. When the ovum implants, about five months after conception, the actual development period (two months) begins. Black bears give birth in late January/ February; grizzly bears in early January/February.

Hibernation

During the late summer and early fall, bears enter *hyperphagia*, the act of eating enormous quantities of food (twenty thousand calories per day) to build up fat. They seek high-calorie foods, including nuts, acorns, and natural sugars (berries and fruits). They also consume great quantities of water. Such activities often require an increase in the bears' travels. Preparation for hibernation is a serious business.

Hibernation is a state of dormancy and inactivity that allows bears to adapt to short winter food supplies. A "true" hibernation period, experienced by bats, squirrels, rodents, and some other animals, is a state of torpidity accompanied by a low metabolic rate and temperatures many degrees below normal. However, during a bear's hibernation, which lasts about five to six months, its body temperature drops only approximately 10 degrees, with its metabolic rate remaining comparatively high. *Bears may awaken during a warm period in the winter and move about outside the den, and some black bears in warmer climates may not hibernate at all.*

Grizzly and black bears begin preparing their dens in September. Black bears begin their hibernation period in early October. Grizzly bears will begin entering their dens in mid-October.

Black bears use existing natural areas for dens—under logs, at the bases or in the cavities of tree roots, under large boulders, in brush piles, and, in some areas, well above ground in trees. Grizzly bears dig their dens under large boulders or tree roots, utilizing this natural structural support.

A den normally houses a single occupant, except when newborns arrive, and the cubs remain with their mother one or two additional winters. Sometimes siblings share quarters for the winter following the separation from their mother.

Motherhood is inaugurated in the den as the pregnant female gives birth in January/February, while in hibernation. One or two cubs are born (the average is two, though three is not uncommon); they weigh less than a pound and measure eight inches long.

The drowsy mother, from the moment of giving birth, begins her long effort to assure her offspring's survival.

The tiny cubs develop rapidly, walking in five to six weeks; black bears weigh five pounds by eight weeks of age, and grizzly bears more than ten pounds. The cubs are nutritionally weaned in twenty-two to twenty-four weeks, but social independence requires a longer period—sixteen to eighteen months for black bears, and up to twenty-nine months for young grizzly bears.

Emerging from Hibernation in Spring

Males and poorly conditioned sows are the first to emerge from hibernation, beginning in late March (emergence during mild winters and springs may be considerably earlier); healthy sows and cubs leave their dens in mid- to late April. The sow emerges ready to protect her young, remaining close to the den, probably acclimatizing the cubs to the outside world.

The emergence process is typically slow and accompanied by sniffing, limping, stretching, limbering of stiff muscles, grooming, yawning, and scratching.

An early concern of emerging bears is water. They are not immediately interested in heavy eating. However, they soon seek high-protein foods—roots, herbs, nuts, old berries left from the fall, and carcasses of animals that have died during the winter.

They begin to resume routine activities, and soon are busy devoting the highest percentage of their time to the search for food. Bears are more naturally diurnal than nocturnal that is; their primary period of activity occurs during daylight hours, though the amount of diurnal activity varies with species, individuals, and environmental influences. The bottom line is that *you may find bears active at any time of the day or night.*

HOW BEARS THINK

BEARS ARE SHY but curious, suspicious, self-reliant, clever, wily, fearless, independent, and dangerous. The only sure things about a bear's complex behavior are that the animal will always seek food and be unpredictable. And, like humans, bears display behaviors unique to individuals.

Black bears are extremely clever, creatures of habit, inquisitive, and playful. They are more easily food conditioned, meaning they more easily become accustomed to seeking and eating human foods and garbage, than the grizzly bear. Grizzly bears are more dignified, deliberate, and fearless; they are generally shy and peaceful, but ferocious when provoked. This is not to say that black bears are not dangerous. Anyone faced with a charging black bear sow protecting her cubs would consider her, at the very least, ferocious.

Bears learn rapidly and are quite capable of reason. Their curiosity, combined with an excellent memory, is the crux of bears' intelligence. They learn and remember from a single experience—the location of a food source, a threat, a trap, or a rifle shot. They display cunning minds; they bluff, choose alternatives, avoid problems, outwit humans, retreat in the face of great odds (human impacts, dominant bears). They are resourceful.

Bears' curiosity may be attributed to many things, but most often a potential meal is the source. They inspect odors, objects, and sometimes noise to determine if the origin is edible or a possible plaything. Unfortunately, their curiosity often brings them into the proximity of people, resulting in encounters and conflicts.

Bears are solitary animals, except for family groups of sows and cubs, or a sibling group that may remain together during first year or two away from the mother. There is a social hierarchy, and they communicate their moods with expressive signals such as posturing, vocalizing, and marking with odors and other sign.

BEAR SIGN

MARKING (SIGNING) is a highly ritualized method of communication between bears, but its specific purpose is not completely understood by humans. The most important thing it tells you is that a bear or bears are or have been in the area.

Specific marking methods may include tree rubbing with a shoulder, neck, head, or rump; tree biting or clawing; pushing a tree over and rubbing on the downed tree; rolling on the ground at the base of a tree; leaving scat or urinating; biting signs or buildings; rubbing on a log; and pawing the ground.

The many theories for the purpose of marking include a display of dominance (hierarchy) that will avoid conflicts injurious to both bears; communication between males and females during the breeding season; identification of a territory; identification of individuals; the expression of belligerence; and simply the expression of boredom, strength, or play.

ENCOUNTERS WITH HUMANS

DURING ITS ANNUAL CYCLE of activities, a bear's activities may be seriously impacted by the people who use bear country. Human developments and activities encroach upon bear habitat. Bears become unafraid of people, habituated, willing to be in close proximity to them; the availability of unnatural foods near people can condition the bears and even attract them to people. People and bears in close proximity means a high potential for encounters that result in property damage, injury, and even death— sometimes of the people, and quite often of the bear.

DIFFERENCES BETWEEN BLACK AND GRIZZLY BEARS

WHEN TRAVELING IN BEAR COUNTRY where both black and grizzly bears live, it is important that you be able to differentiate the individual species. How you should react during an attack will depend to some degree upon whether a grizzly or a black bear is involved. Proper preventive measures also depend on the species.

Distribution

To begin with, you should learn the populations that naturally occur in the area of your travels.

Black Bear Distribution in North America
(Courtesy C. Servheen, USFWS)

Grizzly Bear Distribution in North America
(Courtesy C. Servheen, USFWS)

The American black bear, the most common species, is distributed in forty-two of the contiguous states, and in eleven of the twelve Canadian provinces and territories.

Grizzly bear distribution in the contiguous United States is quite limited—small areas in Idaho, Montana, Washington, and Wyoming. Grizzly bears are considerably more prevalent in Alaska, and in Canada—Alberta, British Columbia, the Northwest Territories, and the Yukon Territory.

Physical Differences

For the most part, physical differences between the species are easy to identify.

SIZE   Grizzly bears are relatively larger (heavier and
            taller) than black bears. For example, adult

Black Bear
(Courtesy Yellowstone National Park)

Grizzly Bear
(Courtesy Yellowstone National Park)

female grizzly bears weigh 1.7 to 2.3 times as much as adult female black bears. Full-grown black bears, however, may be larger than young grizzly bears. Adult male grizzlies are three to five feet tall (at the shoulder while standing on four legs). Adult black bears stand two and a half to three feet high.

HEAD   The face of a black bear displays a straighter profile (between the forehead and nose) and a pronounced forehead, with the ears small, rounded, and set well back on the head. A grizzly bear has a concave (dished) face profile, and its ears are relatively small and located farther forward on the head.

HUMP   Grizzly bears have a hump—a mass of muscle—between their shoulders that is covered with long hair. The long hair often accentuates the hump when the "hackles" are raised. This hump is normally a reliable means of identification; the black bear has no such feature.

FUR   The fur (hair) of the black bear is, over all shorter and of more uniform length. The grizzly bear's is longer and of unequal lengths, giving a "shaggy" appearance.

COLOR   The coloration of the fur is quite variable between the two species *and* within each species. Color is sometimes misleading and possibly the most unreliable means of bear identification.

Black bears occur in numerous shades of brown, including rich chocolate, light, and cinnamon, as well as blond, yellow, silver, and black. The throat or chest is sometimes adorned with a white V-shaped patch. The face is always brownish.

A grizzly bear may be dark brown, almost black, to cream, nearly white. The intensity of color varies over the body. Black hairs usually have white tips; the guard hairs extend beyond the mat of fur and, if pale-tipped, provide a "silvertip" or grizzled appearance. White collars on cubs are not uncommon.

PAW   Black bears have more hair between the toes and foot pad, and more webbing at the base of the toe pad. The claws are distinctively

Grizzly Bear Forepaw
(© Gary Brown)

different between the two species. Those of the black bear are short, hooked, and black in color; grizzly bear claws are large, long, and narrow, only slightly curved, and somewhat blunt. The grizzly bear's foreclaws are four to five inches long and normally strikingly visible. The color is somewhat variable, though often very light.

TRACKS   The black bear's front paw tracks are distinct; toes loosely spaced from a curved arc; claw mark length not more than toe pad length, and often not visible; intermediate, or middle, pad is wedge-shaped; hindpaw track similar to human track; heel pad sometimes not visible.

Grizzly bear tracks are often indistinct; toes

close together (tight-toed) and forming a relatively straight line; toe pads joined; foreclaws' print twice as long as toe pad's; round heel pad sometimes not visible.

Habitat

Black bears are typically forest (conifer, mixed, deciduous) animals, though they move into small open areas to feed.

Grizzly bears use open (arctic tundra and scarcely forested) habitats close to forested areas. They often are

Palmisciano Method
(A Method for Differentiating Black Bear and Grizzly Bear Tracks)
(Illustration from Bear Attacks by Stephen Herrero)

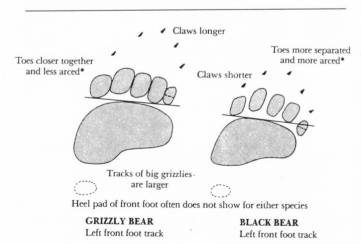

Claws longer

Toes closer together and less arced*

Toes more separated and more arced*

Claws shorter

Tracks of big grizzlies are larger

Heel pad of front foot often does not show for either species

GRIZZLY BEAR
Left front foot track

BLACK BEAR
Left front foot track

found in forested (mixed, conifer, deciduous) areas, where they use the forest meadows and other openings.

Foods

Black bears consume more green vegetation, berries, and seeds, while grizzly bears eat more roots, bulbs and tubers, and vertebrates (animals). Both species are opportunistic feeders and scavengers, and much of their diets is common to both species.

•

Several other major differences that exist between the species require close, in-hand scrutiny to recognize, and I am certain that you would not want to get close enough to find them out. The above description should provide you guidelines adequate to identify the respective bears of both species.

2

Bear Attacks

N ow that you know a bit about bears—how they think, how they act—how do we all get along together in bear country?

To begin with, there exists a broad definition of what constitutes an encounter with a bear. Some people

Grizzly Bear
(Courtesy Yellowstone National Park)

consider nothing short of an all-out attack as an encounter, where others regard an observation of a bear hundreds of yards in the distance as a threatening confrontation. The interpretation will certainly depend upon the individual, the location, and the outcome of the "meeting." Encounters with bears, whether major attacks or close confrontations, are considered either provoked or unprovoked, depending on the source of provocation.

PROVOKED ENCOUNTERS

A VARIETY OF CIRCUMSTANCES influence each encounter, but most are in some way human-controlled. We are capable of intentionally or unintentionally causing an encounter.

Provoked encounters include:

- Feeding or baiting a bear (including improperly storing food or garbage).
- Bears attracted to people due to the odors of human foods, garbage, or other attractants.
- Bears attracted to people having learned them to be a source of food.
- Surprising a bear.
- Posing a threat to a bear by crowding or encroaching into its space. Encounters can result when a bear is protecting a food source or cubs, or when it believes it is cornered and feels trapped.

UNPROVOKED ENCOUNTERS

WHAT WE HUMANS consider an unprovoked encounter *is* always provoked as far as the bear is concerned. Its reason for its actions, though, is not always apparent to us. The bear may have been forced by dominant bears into lesser-quality habitat that is near a road or other areas with human activities. To survive it must then use these areas, remaining in close proximity to people, becoming habituated to them. If the bear receives human foods or is crowded by people, it is placed in a position of potential conflict. Also, a bear may be in such poor physical condition, or may be so starved, that it seeks any possible source of food including human foods and garbage. Its unprovoked actions may be predation. There are documented incidents of bears, mostly black bears, preying on humans.

CAUSES OF
ENCOUNTERS/ATTACKS

ENCOUNTERS OBVIOUSLY OCCUR when people and bears are brought together. Food attractants, surprising a bear, encroaching upon a bear's space, and appearing as a threat to a sow with cubs are the primary culprits. The causes may be multiple and complex, however, with several determining the actual encounter and — most importantly—the outcome.

Attractants

Human foods and garbage naturally entice these opportunistic feeders. Other attractants include foods intended for consumption by pets and livestock, along with their related garbage and a variety of other odorous items, including cosmetics, insect repellents, and toothpaste. All are of major interest to a gluttonous bear, and if they are not properly stored and secured the bear will be rewarded.

Bears that are allowed to obtain these foods, either intentionally (feeding) or unintentionally (inadequate security), become *food conditioned*—reliant upon this easily obtainable food. Their amazing memories allow them to become conditioned after only a single event and they will certainly return to these "easy pickings."

Habituation

Bears, though naturally cautious, may become *habituated* to people if exposed to frequent non-threatening contacts. If a bear returns often to food sources that are in close proximity to people it will lose its timidity. Its willingness to closely approach or be in the vicinity of human activity, greatly enhances the chances for a human/bear confrontation. Black bears are especially prone to becoming habituated to human development and activities.

Surprise

Surprising a bear is the most common cause of an attack. This is unnecessary, because surprising a bear is, in most situations, preventable. Bears are normally shy and most often flee when aware of people. However, people who move silently through bear country without letting their presence be known at a distance, and who fail to be alert to their surroundings, can find themselves in a close confrontation, causing a bear to perceive a threat to itself, its cubs, or a guarded food source. The result is known as a serious surprise encounter.

Invasion of Critical Space

How do you feel when someone talks to you with his face only six inches away from yours? Uncomfortable? That person has invaded your "critical space." Bears, like humans, have a "space," an area about them in which they are not comfortable when others encroach. A bear's critical space may be twenty feet or a quarter mile—nearly any distance, depending on the individual bear and circumstances. In other words, you can't begin to guess what the space is. You have to instead warn a bear so that it can flee.

A bear protecting a food source, especially a large cache such as a deer or elk carcass, will defend its prize when it feels threatened. Also, an intrusion into the protective space of a sow with cubs nearly always results in a major

A Grizzly Bear Reacts to Being Crowded in its Critical Space
(© Gary Brown)

confrontation. And as you might imagine, a sow with cubs feeding on a carcass could be considered double jeopardy.

When a bear is approached too closely, whatever the distance, its reaction to the encroachment will depend on its individual temperament. It may display a nonaggressive response or, in many such situations, an aggressive one. Whatever the reaction, it will not necessarily be due to surprise. The bear may have been well aware of you for some time, but wasn't bothered until you violated its area of comfort.

Protection of Young

A sow with cubs is typically the most dangerous bear. The normally placid but extremely alert mother bear considers motherhood—the education and protection of her cubs—as her paramount objective. There is a deep family bond. The mother is affectionate, devoted,

Grizzly Bear Sow with Two Cubs
(Courtesy Yellowstone National Park)

and constantly protective (aggressive toward threats, real or perceived). She defends her cubs to whatever degree she believes necessary, bluffing or attacking until she has lessened the threat to her young. Nothing prompts a full-blown charge by a bear more quickly than the bawl and commotion of a cub.

A BEAR ATTACK

BEAR ATTACKS, the ultimate encounters, are uncommon, though several occur in North America each year. They are most often provoked by people who have set the stage for the tragedy. Some result in only minor injuries, but the vast majority result in serious physical and mental trauma, some ending in death.

Every encounter with a bear is a potential attack. The difference between a bear fleeing when aware of your presence, and attacking and mauling you (and every situation in between), is only a matter of degree.

The attack by a bear, an all-out aggressive charge and actual contact, has been described by several victims as awesome, and of course absolutely terrifying. The speed with which the bear is upon its victim is unbelievable. It may charge at 30 to 35 mph, leaving you with minimal time to think and consider your options. The bear's movements while attacking are extremely quick; it uses its forepaws to strike with enormous strength and power, biting the victims' heads and necks. An attacking bear is capable of knocking you ten to fifteen feet away, and then being upon you before you come to a stop. This combination of quickness and power is unparalleled in the wild. But, as the mauling occurs, the victims' senses are heightened and everything is perceived in slow motion. They smell the bear, its breath, hear the breathing and the damaging actions of the bears, see each individual hair of the bear's fur, its eyes. The squeals of the cubs, if involved, are vivid, and often further excite the attacking bear.

At this point, let us review a few bear attacks that have occurred during the past dozen or so years. I have used fictitious names, but the events are accurate according to the subjects and investigators.

George, who was hiking alone, silently except for the sound of his boots striking the ground, raised his eyes from his almost continuous gaze at the trail to see the staring face of a sow grizzly bear approximately eighty feet distant. At her side were two yearling cubs. George swiftly ran twelve feet to a tree—and the sow reached him at the same moment he arrived there. Only biting his arm, she returned to her cubs and watched him for a short period. There was no further display of aggressive behavior, and she departed with her offspring.

(An example of surprising a bear at close range—crowding it—and of a sow "lessening the threat" to her cubs.)

❖

Jake was also hiking alone, off-trail and silently, when he smelled something dead. At that moment he observed a large grizzly bear running directly at him. Before he could move it knocked him over backward, pounced on him, and began biting his abdomen and chest. He was eventually able to roll over and assume a position of playing dead. The bear hesitated momentarily, then renewed its attack—biting and clawing him on the buttocks, back, and top of the head—before running off a short distance. Jake could hear a grunting and "woofing" sound, and when he moved slightly, the bear returned. Again, he was clawed and bitten along his back, receiving further deep punctures and tearing-type wounds. After what Jake believed to be at least a minute (probably only a few seconds), the bear ceased the onslaught and left the area. Jake, barely capable of walking, managed to reach a road where he found assistance. He has since recovered, except for serious scarring and considerable recurring mental trauma.

(An example of violating the space of a bear guarding a food source—carrion—and possibly of surprising the bear at close range.)

Jim had left the backcountry trail on which he was hiking when he apparently surprised a grizzly bear at very close range. He immediately attempted to climb a tree, but had proceeded only a few inches upward when the bear grabbed him with its mouth and dragged him to the ground. He was deeply bitten about the head and upper body. When he played dead, the bear left the area and he was able to reach a trailhead where assistance was available.

(An example of surprising a bear and of the value of playing dead.)

Sara, age six, was camping with her parents in a developed, drive-in campground. Not long after the family had retired for the night, Sara left the tent and, without a flashlight, proceeded to the nearby rest room. As she was returning to the campsite in the darkness, a bear (species unidentified) grabbed her by the chest with its mouth and lifted her off the ground, shaking her like a rag doll. The bear dropped her and fled when other campers responded to the situation.

(An example of a habituated and probably food-conditioned bear being surprised in a developed area, in the darkness, and approached too closely by a person without a flashlight or other light source.)

Two young girls were hiking at the top of a relatively open hillside above a summer resort area. The lakeshore vacation neighborhood had a history of black bears prowling and getting into garbage cans. The hill where the girls were walking had some scattered trees and patches of dense brush. Mary and Alice both heard a noise in the brush, turned to look, and found a bear four or five feet away. Screaming, they ran across the hill, but Alice quickly altered her course and proceeded downhill. Mary heard a "strange" scream, and then silence. She hid in some brush for a short time, and, when she didn't hear or see anything, ran to a home to seek assistance. The first people to reach the area near the hilltop found only Alice's swim shorts. A short time later, a larger search party found blood and a torn blouse. The searchers began combing the hillside and soon found the bear three hundred yards from the clothing items, "guarding" the dead girl's terribly mauled body. The bear chased one searcher up a tree before it was killed. The 250-pound black bear was examined and found to be healthy.

(Probably an example of a bear that was habituated to people but surprised and crowded at a close distance. Running may have triggered its instinct to chase.)

I have described these encounters/attacks not to sensationalize, but to emphasize that bears must be taken seriously and respected for what they are—large and powerful wild animals. *It behooves you to prevent an encounter!*

3

Avoiding
Bear Encounters
(Attacks)

BEFORE YOU LEAVE HOME—
PLANNING

S afe travel in bear country begins long before you ever leave home. One of the most important ingredients in preventing bear attacks is your preparation for the proposed trip and its specific activities. Biologist and bear expert Stephen Herrero says, "Your best weapon to minimize the risk of a bear attack is your brain. Use it as soon as you contemplate a trip to bear country, and continue to use it throughout your stay."

Proper preparation for your adventure into bear country can not only save your life, but can itself be an enjoyable and rewarding aspect of the trip. Your research may enhance your knowledge of the area, its natural and cultural histories, and its features of interest.

Be flexible, though. You may need to alter your initial plans when you receive additional information about your proposed destination.

First, consider the means by which you are traveling in bear country: conventional automobile or truck, four-wheel-drive vehicle, recreational vehicle, all terrain vehicle (ATV), bicycle, motorcycle, canoe, boat, raft, skis, snowshoes, snow machine, or foot. Your mode of transportation dictates your equipment, your supplies, your overnight accommodations, and *how* you safely travel in bear country. For example, if you are staying in a cabin or lodge, your planning and travels will be considerably different than if you are hiking and camping in the backcountry: Food security at a lodge is definitely simpler than it is in a backcountry campsite. Still, even if you are eating at restaurants or other food facilities, you have a food security concern and responsibility. If one of your activities as a lodge guest is hiking in bear country, you must be as prepared as a backpacker.

Philosophy of Traveling in Bear Country

Wild areas, pieces of country with wildlife including bears, are special and intriguing to many. When you share these areas with those who were there first—the bears—you leave behind many of the safeguards of your civilized life. There is no guarantee of your safety. *You accept a risk when you are in bear country*—a risk that adds an element of excitement and wildness to your travel enjoyment. Anyone unable to accept this risk should not travel in bear country. Accepting the risk means accepting the responsibility for your conduct in bear country—and acting in a way that protects you, members of your travel party, and bears.

Attitude

Your attitude may be the key to preventing a bear attack. The attitude that "it can not happen to me, those things always happen to someone else" can be disastrous. The person who is cocky, who challenges bear country and its inhabitants, is, simply put, "asking for" a major encounter.

Your best approach is to respect the country and, specifically, the bears. Honor their home and their ability to be devastating hosts. Do not expect to be protected by the land managers, the agencies, or others. Many agencies provide excellent bear information, but most have inadequate funding and staffs, and expect you to be prepared to prevent bear attacks. The responsibility is upon your shoulders.

Knowledge and Information about Bear Country

As you develop your travel plans, gather as much information as possible about the areas you will visit. Knowledge about bears in general is important, but understanding the bears of your specific destination is critical. Learn to identify both species, and be able to recognize bear sign (see pages 23-24). Know the areas bears utilize during the particular season in which you'll be traveling. Also, learn the outdoor skills you'll need: camping, vehicle travel, hiking, anything related to your proposed activities. But most of all, remember that the more you know about bears, the better your chances of avoiding an encounter.

Aggressively seek out information. You can use the following sources. You should also listen to the advice of rangers and wildlife managers, ask questions, and carefully read all handouts and other available sources of information.

READ

Read everything you are able to obtain about bears. The recommended reading list at the back of this book is a general foundation, but much more specific bear information relative to your destination is available.

Field guides will provide extremely important details for recognizing the different species as well as bear sign.

AGENCIES/CHAMBERS OF COMMERCE

Contact the information sources of the respective management agencies and local chambers of commerce in your destination area by mail, telephone, or FAX. Even some of your hometown travel agents will have general information, though it may downplay any dangers, so as not to discourage sales.

Land management agencies will normally provide the most thorough and accurate facts. Also, they can tell you which permits, if any, are necessary for use of an area.

FISH AND GAME DEPARTMENTS

Communications with your local wildlife management department should provide you with information about bears and their habitat, and even enhance your knowledge of bear sign (see pages 23-24). They may have exhibits that will aid in species identification.

AUDIOVISUAL PROGRAMS

Your hometown organizations and agencies often have public wildlife programs that cover, among other wild animals, bears, as well as other natural and cultural features that may figure in your travel plans.

National parks and forests, chambers of commerce, and even city information bureaus offer a variety of programs, such as formal talks and guided trips, that reflect on safe travel in the local bear country.

VIDEOTAPES

Rent any of the excellent bear documentary videos available at your local video store. They will assist in the identification of species and bear sign, as well as provide knowledge of bear behavior.

EXPERIENCED TRAVELERS

Discuss traveling in bear country with friends or others who travel, camp, or hike where there are bears. Glean any information possible from them, and learn from their experiences. Have they had any encounters with bears? Why? Can you prevent that type of encounter? What did they do correctly or incorrectly?

ZOOS/WILDLIFE PARKS

Visit a wildlife park or zoo to observe bears. (If you are experienced in bear country, this will be an excellent refresher course.) Learn to identify the bear species. Nearly every wildlife facility has American black and brown (grizzly) bears. Watch their behavior—even though this is a captive situation, you will increase your familiarity with bears.

TRAVEL GROUP

At the outset of the trip, discuss bears and specific travel plans with those in your travel group. These are the people whose actions in bear country are as important as your own in preventing encounters. Your own actions in bear country may be perfect, but if your companions are careless you will suffer right along with them. Each member of a travel party must be responsible and assist others in doing the same.

GUIDED HIKES

Participate in guided hikes in bear country. These are often excellent means of experiencing and learning about safe travel. You will benefit firsthand from the knowledge of experienced bear country travelers. Be certain, however, that the organization is experienced and legitimate.

Bear Attractants

The nose of a bear is its fundamental link with its environment. An old and often-related Native American saying may best describe the sensitive nose of a bear: "A pine needle fell in the forest. The eagle saw it. The deer heard it. The bear smelled it."

Because bears are omnivorous, they are attracted to just about any potential food source. They are drawn to anything that smells like food (natural or unnatural), to chemical odors, and in many situations to unfamiliar odors. And, of course these attractants exist wherever people do.

Not only will a bear be attracted to these food sources, it will consume them, and is capable of damaging anything in its way and injuring you in the process. The attractant does not have to be large. Even a tiny scrap of food on the ground can lead a bear to a location. Sometimes, too, a bear is attracted to an accumulation of odors in which no specific item is evident or detectible by you: small decaying bits and scraps of foods in a campsite, picnic area, or cabin that over time become an attractant. Your camping and cooking equipment may also collect food odors or other alluring scents over time.

As a traveler in bear country, *an understanding of what interests and attracts bears is essential to you*, and should be a major consideration in your planning as well as throughout your trip. Be able to recognize the attractants, and know what measures to take (listed below) to minimize them. *Before your trip plan carefully* to eliminate any article that might attract a bear.

Foods that Attract Bears

- All foods, including canned foods, other commercially packaged items, grease, and beverages (canned or bottled pop, beer).
- Food leftovers.
- Gum, candy, snacks.
- All pet and livestock foods (including empty food and water bowls, and bird feeders and feed), and all of their accompanying odors.

PREVENTION

- Do not carry fresh foods.
- Do not carry highly odorous foods (like bacon, sausage, cheese, fish, or fresh meats).
- Select lightweight foods that require minimal storage space and can be readily raised to a secure location in the backcountry (see *Hanging Attractants* under *Food Storage—The Campground*, page 84-85.)
- Freeze-dried foods are relatively odor-free and commonly used in bear country; consider the type that is cooked in its own pouch, therefore eliminating the need to wash pots.
- Make sure your food is packaged airtight; use zipper-lock-type plastic bags.
- Predetermine portions per package so you will have no leftovers.
- Keep the exteriors of food packages clean.
- Repackaging foods is sometime necessary, so carry extra plastic bags or other airtight containers.

- Never bring bird feeders or bird feed.
- Keep food items neat, orderly, and clean.
- *Careful food planning is critical.*

Cooking Equipment that Attracts Bears

- Food containers (full or empty), including icechests, coolers, and thermoses. Food containers retain odors, even after thorough cleansing; also, they are visible targets for bears.
- All beverage containers (water or other drinks).
- Cooking and eating utensils (pots, stoves, dishes, etc.) retain odors.
- Grills, barbecues, and hibachis.

Grizzly Bear Eating
Unsecured Campground Garbage
(Courtesy Yellowstone National Park)

PREVENTION

- Prior to your trip, wash all food storage and preparation items (dishes, bowls, pots, etc.), as well as eating utensils to minimize odors.
- Use a stove (liquid petroleum or gasoline type) instead of building a cooking fire.

Garbage and Trash that Attract Bears

- All garbage and trash, regardless of the amount, including apparently clean wrappers.

PREVENTION

- Appropriately handle and dispose of all your garbage and trash, securing from bears (see pages 88-92). Backcountry users should pack out all materials, therefore plastic bags are essential.

Wastewater that Attracts Bears

- Dishwater and excess cooking water are highly odorous attractants.

PREVENTION

- Proper methods of disposing of wastewater are described under *Camp and Area Sanitation* on pages 81-84.

Tent, Clothing, Sleeping Bag, and Other Camp Equipment

- Camp equipment and your clothing (especially clothes worn while cooking) collect food odors.

- Water pails, buckets, and wash basins collect odors.
- Camp tables and chairs accumulate food scraps and odors.
- Backpacks normally have attracting odors.
- Food smells permeate your tent, sleeping bag, and other equipment.

PREVENTION

- Wash or clean all of your equipment, including your tent and pack, before you begin your trip; this may be critical if you have cooked in or near it.
- Carry enough clothing so that you don't need to sleep in the same clothes in which you cook and eat.

Personal Cleanliness

- Various odors (food, medicines, lotions, repellents, etc.) that linger on your body may attract bears.
- Human sexual activity may attract bears.

PREVENTION

- Keep as personally clean as possible.
- Plan to washup well after cooking, eating, or sex, and before retiring.

Other Odorous Items That Attract Bears

- Perfumes, deodorants, cosmetics, lotions, shampoos, soaps, suntan lotions, toothpaste, and sweet-smelling substances.
- Scented toiletries.
- Some first-aid items and medicines (Campho-Phenique has been known to attract a bear).

- Lip salves and balms.
- Insect repellents.
- Pot scrubbers.
- Vinyl, foam rubber, motor oil.
- Most any scented or flavored item.

PREVENTION

- Bring unscented toiletries when possible.
- Do not bring along any more of the above items than necessary.
- Carefully pack them in airtight containers, and appropriately store them at your destination (hang with your food, keep in a hard-sided vehicle, or secure in a building).

Recognizing Bear Sign

The recognition of bear sign is one of the most critical elements of preventing an encounter with a bear. It also adds a wonderful new dimension to the natural history lessons of your trip. Bear sign comes in many forms, some readily recognizable and others more subtle and difficult to detect. It may be on the ground, a tree, a building, or another object. Before leaving home, study and learn how to recognize the various signs left by bears.

Bear sign includes:

TRACKS   Tracks will be one of the primary signs you encounter in bear country; often there will be just partial tracks, and bears will not always leave visible tracks if the ground surface is dry and hard; the track of a bear will be five-toed, generally as long as a human's footprint but twice as wide, and

Grizzly Bear Scat
(Courtesy Yellowstone National Park)

with claw marks extended beyond the toes. (See *Differences Between Black and Grizzly Bears*—Tracks, page 29.)

SCAT   Bear feces are often found on a trail, though they may be observed anywhere; the scat is a mass of partly digested grasses, acorns, berries, insects, seeds, hair, pieces of bone, roots, wood pulp, fruits, etc.; the average sizes of scat are roughly 2 1/4" (adult grizzly bear) and 1 3/8" (adult black bear) in diameter, though size overlap occurs.

LOGS   Old, rotten logs and stumps are torn apart or rolled over in search of ants or other insects.

ROCKS   Rocks are overturned for the insects beneath

them; most obvious are those rocks lying on green vegetation adjacent to a bare area.

CLAW MARKS AND TEETH MARKS   Trees, buildings, signs, and trail tags are often climbed, scratched, or bitten by bears as a means of "marking" (a highly ritualized function of communication); on "bear trees" there are vertical scratch marks (claws), and bite marks, sometimes as high as twelve feet up; bears may destroy signs and break into buildings.

DIGGING   Bears consume considerable quantities of foods (roots, worms, insects, small vertebrates) found below the surface of the ground, therefore meadows and other open areas often have excavations; sometimes just the sod is turned over, or sometimes large areas are excavated to a considerable depth in the pursuit of rodents and squirrels; anthills are torn apart or dug out; scooped-out depressions (claw marks often visible) in dry stream banks may be the sign of a bear digging out the nests of swallows; any evidence of digging in grizzly bear country is probably grizzly bear sign.

GRAZING   Areas where there are missing flower heads may be signs of bear grazing.

CACHES   Bears cover the carcasses of animals (carrion) and carefully guard them; these caches normally appear as humps on the ground with tree branches, dirt, and grasses covering the prize, and may strongly smell of a dead animal; a secondary sign associated with the cache might be a gathering of scavenging birds such as ravens, magpies, jays, and eagles.

FISH PARTS The remnants of fish—heads, tails, eggs—are commonly seen along streams where bears have been feeding on a spawn; the odor of dead and rotting fish may also be evident.

HAIR Bears rub against trees, leaving hair imbedded in the bark or stuck in the flowing pitch; hair may also be found on brush, fences, buildings, or most anywhere a bear has rubbed or closely passed by.

STRIPPED BARK Bears will strip down and tear off the bark of a tree to eat the inner (cambium) layer; you may find hair in the flowing pitch; stripped bark may also be a sign of antlered and horned wildlife, which often rub their heads against trees.

BEAR TRAILS Bears often follow the same route so often that that a definite trail develops; if they repeatedly step in their own tracks, depressions often develop where each paw has been placed.

DAY BEDS You may locate a day bed, a depression in the ground (lots of scat nearby), where a bear or bears rest when not feeding or traveling; day beds are often near a food source.

Bark Stripped From a Tree by a Bear
(Courtesy Yellowstone National Park)

A BEAR   This is the most authentic sign of bear activity.

There are several excellent resources listed in Chapter 6, Recommended Reading, that will assist you in identifying tracks and other bear sign. Also, look for field guides covering your travel area and other publications with bear sign information specific to that location.

Transportation/Overnight Accommodations

Decide which type of transportation and overnight accommodations you will be using prior to embarking upon your travels. Your options are generally based on your interests and activities. You may travel by conventional automobile or truck, four-wheel-drive vehicle, all terrain vehicle (ATV), bicycle, motorcycle, hiking, canoe, boat, raft, skis, snowshoes, or snow machine. Overnight accommodations may be a motel, lodge, tent, under-the-stars, travel trailer, truck camper, motor home, pop-up (folding tent) trailer, or pop-up camper. Your activities may include hiking, camping in front or backcountry, snow camping, fishing, bicycling, or any combination of these activities. Each of these methods of travel and activities is addressed in the section *Travels in Bear Country* later in this chapter.

Vehicle Travel

There are bear attractants in every vehicle. Most often foods—including snacks, drinks, even a single piece of gum or candy, and the leftover packaging and crumbs of these items—are found in vehicles, especially if children are in the travel group. The vehicle's glove box often contains attractants (food, gum, toiletries), and vehicle trunks may have food odors since that is where groceries and travel/camping supplies are normally carried. A thorough interior cleaning of your vehicle is advisable before your trip into bear country. Bears have broken windows or torn off doors of vehicles to obtain food (though this is quite rare).

Some vehicles are not bear resistant, including convertibles and soft-sided Jeep-types with canvas or vinyl tops and sides. Some recreational conveyances, such as four-wheel-drive backcountry vehicles, are even opensided. Obviously, this type of construction will not deter a bear seeking food, and it is therefore impossible to properly secure attractants within these vehicles. The back of pickups and some other types of trucks are not secure from bears, and vehicle top racks, of either open or solid construction, are not bear resistant.

Consider your camping facility and method as carefully as your type of vehicle. Soft-sided units, such as tents, pop-up campers, and pop-up tent trailers, are vulnerable to bears seeking foods. Odors in these units are easily detected and entry through the soft sides is quite simple for a bear, and has even occurred while a unit was occupied. I advise you not to tent camp (including camping in pop-up campers and pop-up trailers) in areas where bear activity is high; you definitely should not if you are unable to properly secure your foods from bears.

Do not free camp (under the stars, without a tent or other shelter) in bear country, even if your food is appropriately secured. Passing bears have been known to inspect sleepers, pawing and biting the exposed head and face.

In some bear country campgrounds the managing agency prohibits both the use of soft-sided camping units (tents, pop-up trailers, and pop-up campers) and free camping; only hard-sided camping is allowed.

Before you leave home, plan the method(s) you will use to store foods and other bear attractants.

Before you leave home, carefully consider your transportation and overnight accommodations, and the activities you might engage in during your travels. Plan the method(s), and acquire the necessary equipment and materials, you will use to store foods and other bear attractants (refer to *Bear Attractants*, pages 51-56).

Regardless of your activities, foods should be stored in air-tight, zipper-lock-type plastic bags.

If you are going to hang your attractants to secure them from bears, you must have available the following items:

- Small, air-tight, plastic bags (preferably zipper-lock-type) for food, and garbage and trash.
- Two fifty-foot lengths of quality, lightweight, high-strength, 1/8 to 1/4 inch cord or rope.
- Stuff bags (nylon type) or other containers that can be hoisted with the attractants that must be secured.

Backcountry Travel

Traveling into the backcountry, whether as a short or day hike, or as an overnight adventure, provides an experience of freedom and self-reliance. However, you are entering the area of bear country where surprise encounters most often occur, and the measures necessary to avoid an encounter with a bear are thus more exacting and laborious.

Do Not Travel Alone

It is strongly advisable to travel in a group of at least three people, preferably four, regardless of the nature of the hike—day use or overnight. The larger the group the more potential for conversation, and the noise of additional clothing rustling or boots on the trail will aid in preventing a surprise encounter. Also, the safety of each individual is enhanced by numbers—more eyes and ears are present to detect bears or bear sign. If there is a problem, whatever the cause, there are more people to attend to the injured hiker while someone summons assistance. Plan together, using the collective brain power of the group, even for a spontaneous day or short hike.

Travel Light

Think *lightweight* if you are backpacking—this is one of the keys to backcountry travel. The fewer pounds (and even ounces) that you carry, the less fatigued you will be during the trip and upon arrival at your destination, and the better able to perceive your surroundings and make proper decisions. Also, you will have less material to secure against bears.

Make Noise

Plan a system for alerting bears of your presence, such as talking, clapping hands, singing, shaking a can filled with pebbles, or using a whistle, bells, or other instrument of sound that will carry in case you tire of conversation. Use a variety of noises.

Properly Store Food

Be prepared to appropriately store your food and other attractants. Carry two fifty-feet pieces of cord or rope, plastic bags that can be sealed, and stuff sacks with which to hang your food.

Special bear-resistant, backpacker food storage canisters are an excellent means to store foods and other attractants away from bears. The canisters are cylinders twelve to eighteen inches long, eight inches in diameter, and made of a hard vinyl material. They weigh three to five pounds. One end is permanently sealed and the other has a recessed lid with a bear-proof latch system.

Hanging Backpack with Attractants
(Courtesy Yellowstone National Park)

They fit nicely into backpacks and are available for purchase or rent, but are often provided free by agencies when you acquire your backcountry use permit. They will need to be hung along with other containers, but in treeless areas they do provide efficient bear-resistant storage when left on the ground (see *Food Storage* pages 83-88, later in this chapter).

To reduce or eliminate attracting odors, wash or clean your tent, sleeping bag, pack, stuff bags, outdoor clothing, and all other equipment between trips.

Physical Condition

Healthy physical condition is important to any bear country travelers, but it is *critical* to hikers, regardless of the distance they hike and whether they are day hiking or camping in the backcountry.

To begin with, if you are in a physical condition that allows you to hike a few miles without approaching exhaustion, you will have a more enjoyable experience. But more importantly, to safely travel in bear country you must be mentally alert. An acute awareness of your actions and environment is essential. You must never forget that you are in bear country—you are sharing the territory with large, powerful animals. It is imperative that you detect their presence and respond in the appropriate manner to prevent an encounter. Your decisions and actions must be based upon well-developed knowledge (gained in advance of the trip) and clear thinking.

There is a definite correlation between your physical and your mental condition. A physically exhausted person is less alert and aware, with impaired judgement and decision-making ability. You may carelessly walk into a confrontation with a bear, or foolishly risk taking a route near a bear because it provides the shortest distance to your destination. You should have the physical ability to alter your route and hike many extra miles if a bear is present.

Emergency Planning

An important element in your planning is the consideration of an emergency. You must have a plan.

Leave your itinerary with family or friends—people who care, who will notify the appropriate authorities if you are overdue from your trip.

As many members of your travel group as possible should have a basic knowledge of first aid, and at least one well-considered and -supplied first-aid/medical kit should be carried.

Register at ranger stations or trailheads if you are traveling into the backcountry, even if only for a day hike. Obtain any necessary use permits.

Ten Basic Principles of Safe Travel in Bear Country

1. *PLAN YOUR TRIP WELL*

   Prepare for your travels in bear country by gaining knowledge of bears and their environment, and learning how to prevent an encounter. *Plan what you will do in the event of a bear encounter.*

2. **BE MENTALLY ALERT**

   Use your brain. Be alert and acutely aware of your actions and the environment in which you are traveling. Accept the fact that there is risk involved in traveling in bear country. Be physically prepared.

3. **CHOOSE APPROPRIATE LOCATIONS AND ROUTES OF TRAVEL**

   Avoid high bear use areas. Do not hike, camp, or stay in an area where bear activity has been reported or there have been recent unresolved bear problems. Be flexible—select another route, destination, or activity.

4. **DO NOT SURPRISE A BEAR**

   Surprising a bear is the most common cause of an attack. But remember, surprise is preventable in most situations.

5. **DO NOT APPROACH A BEAR FOR ANY REASON**

   The encroachment into a bear's critical space, whether the bear is relaxing or protecting cubs or a food source, may result in an encounter. Do not crowd, pursue, or approach any bear for any reason. Critical space varies with individual bears from a few feet to several hundred yards.

6. **RECOGNIZE BEAR SIGN**

   Study field guides and other publications and be able to accurately detect any evidence of bear activity. The presence of bear sign should heighten your alertness and increase your precautionary measures, lessening the chances of an encounter.

7. *CONTROL BEAR ATTRACTANTS*
   Minimize the use of highly odorous foods and other items that might attract a bear to you.

8. *PREVENT BEARS FROM OBTAINING YOUR FOOD AND OTHER ATTRACTANTS*
   Properly store your foods, garbage, and other odorous items at all times, day or night, except when they are being transported, prepared, or used.

9. *DO NOT FEED BEARS*
   Under no circumstances should you feed bears, or any wildlife. "Feeding" is not just intentionally providing foods, garbage or other attractants, but also inadvertently allowing bears to receive food rewards.

10. *ENJOY BEAR COUNTRY*
    Understand and respect bears, appreciating their long association with people. Conduct yourself in a manner that protects you, your property, and the future of bears.

ARRIVAL IN BEAR COUNTRY

THERE IS NORMALLY an abundance of written and verbal bear information available at your destination, and near the trailhead if you are bound for the backcountry, containing local regulations, restrictions, and specific bear warnings.

Though you obtained considerable information before you left home, seek out this material. It will add to your education and to the safety and pleasure of your adventure.

Chambers of commerce, ranger stations, and wildlife management agencies are excellent sources of information. Some of your activities, especially backcountry use, will require permits that themselves include information. Orientations are often provided—sometimes required—at the permit issuing station. Check bulletin / information boards, and attend any naturalist talks or guided walks provided in the area. Read and heed signs advising or warning about bear activities.

Trails and areas may be closed due to bear activity. Closures are for your safety as well as for the benefit of the natural resources, including bears, so do not enter closed-off areas. Often the closure or restriction is based on past occurences or potential human/bear conflicts.

Locals and other people using an area—such as employees and patrons of outdoors shops, and the people behind lodge and motel registration desks—may also be excellent sources of information about bears.

This effort at the beginning of your adventure will take time. But no matter how anxious you are to get going, the knowledge you gain in the local area, when combined with all of your preparatory planning, may be essential in preventing an encounter with a bear.

CLOSED

AREA BEHIND THIS SIGN IS CLOSED TO HUMAN TRAVEL

DANGEROUS BEAR

Department of Interior
National Park Service

A Closure—Dangerous Bear
(Courtesy Yellowstone National Park)

TRAVEL IN BEAR COUNTRY

Roadside and Picnic Areas

Bears along the roadside, including those that frequent picnic areas and roadside turnouts, are habituated to people and conditioned to human foods. They are dangerous wild animals, even though they may appear gentle and willing to approach you. You must take appropriate actions to avoid an encounter.

- Do not stop along the road or in any area where a bear is present.

- *Never* feed a bear.
- Be cautious during any stop, even if no bear is present; an animal may not make its presence known until you have stopped or even set up your picnic meal.
- Keep your windows rolled up whether you are in or out of the vehicle.
- Do not leave your food unattended, even for "only a second."
- If a bear makes an appearance, pick up your food and equipment, place everything in your vehicle, and leave.
- Do not approach a bear, even if it appears "friendly."
- Keep your picnic area clean; do not drop food scraps, and clean up thoroughly when you are finished.
- Deposit your garbage and trash in the often provided bear-resistant trash receptacle.

Staying Overnight

Lodging Area (Hotel, Motel, Cabin, Lodge)

These developed areas, though not necessarily wild backcountry, are often frequented by bears that are conditioned to human foods. There is the potential for lodge and motel guests to encounter a bear as they move about within the lodging areas or participate in other activities, including backcountry travels or just short hikes outside the developed areas. You must always remember that this is bear country.

The Campground

Campgrounds with vehicle access are located along highways and other paved roads, and in the backcountry where they are accessed by unpaved forest roads or in some cases by four-wheel-drive Jeep roads. Those in the front country are the most common and heavily used by people, but bears may frequent any campground.

Ninety percent of the human encounters with bears in these popular campgrounds have been caused by inadequate storage of foods and other attractants. Ice chests are sought out and easily obtained by bears. Tents are readily entered and a camper may not be aware of the danger associated with these nighttime, and sometimes daytime, campground visitors. The results are property damage, personal injury, and ruined vacations (though for nonvictims the sight of a bear is often considered the highlight of their trip). Another result of improper food storage is diminishing bear populations, since bears that are conditioned to human foods and come into dangerous contact with people are often destroyed.

Upon your arrival at a campground, take time to carefully set up camp. Read bulletin boards and information signs for bear warnings and ask the campground attendants (if available) about bears. Be aware of bear sign.

Not all campgrounds practice good bear management. If there is evidence of bear activity in the campground; if there seems to be no enforcement of food security regulations; if garbage receptacles are not bear resistant or overflow with trash; if trash and garbage are abundant in fire pits and elsewhere throughout the campsites; or there is smell of carrion—move on. Camp elsewhere, especially if you are tent camping.

When you select a campsite, there are precautionary measures to take regarding cooking, food storage, sanitation, personal cleanliness, and so on that will reduce the likelihood of an encounter with a bear. These are outlined in this chapter. However, the established size, layout, and configuration of the campground and individual campsite may limit your ability to effectively minimize the risk of an encounter. Accomplish as much as possible.

SELECTING A CAMPSITE

Whether you are camping in a drive-in campground or a backpacker camp, *always arrive at your campsite before dark*. Selecting and organizing your camp, as well as securing your food and other attractants from bears, is considerably easier and more efficient in the daylight.

Where you camp is extremely important. Unfortunately, many campsites are designated, therefore limiting your options. When you select your own campsite there are numerous ways to minimize the potential for a bear encounter. If you are using a campground that has established cabins, tent cabins, huts, or other shelters, you can adapt the outlined measures to your specific situation.

- Take time to properly set up and organize your camp.
- Separate your sleeping area by at least one hundred yards from food preparation and storage area. (You do not want a bear prowling about your tent while investigating odors of food or other attractants.)

Avoid Confrontation
(Courtesy Yellowstone National Park)

WARNING

BEAR

FREQUENTING AREA

Removal of this sign may result in INJURY to others
and is punishable by law

THERE IS NO GUARANTEE OF YOUR SAFETY
WHILE HIKING OR CAMPING IN BEAR COUNTRY

(Courtesy Yellowstone National Park)

- Avoid areas of high bear use, such as locations with good bear foods (berry patches, spawning streams, acorns or nutcrops on the ground, etc.).
- Avoid areas with the smell of dead animals, including dead and rotting fish remnants.
- Do not camp where there is fresh bear sign, such as tracks and/or scat.

- Select a campsite away from hiking or wildlife trails.
- Do not camp directly adjacent to streams, lakes, or ponds, which are often used by bears as travel routes.
- Select a campsite that is in a relatively open area but has some escape trees (with low branches for quick climbing). Avoid dense vegetation, where you have poor visibility and where bears often prefer to remain when investigating unknowns.
- Avoid camps where previous occupants' signs—dirty

Campsite Organization
(© Paricia Brown)

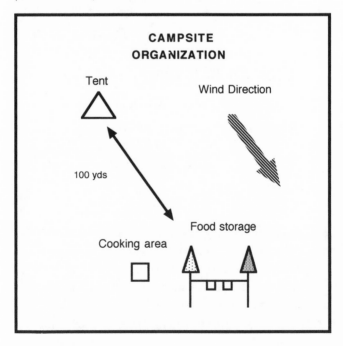

camps, garbage and trash left available to bears—are still apparent; those ahead of you may have developed food-conditioned and habituated bears.

- Do not camp where a campsite has been ransacked by a bear.
- If there are careless campers nearby, suggest good camping practices to them; if there are no improvements, adjust your itinerary and move on even if you are tired. *This is another important reason for arriving at your destination early, with plenty of daylight remaining.*

SLEEPING ARRANGEMENTS

- Place your tent upwind and at least one hundred yards away from your food storage and cooking area (this will not be feasible in most organized drive-in campgrounds, and may also be difficult in some backcountry campsites due to topography and vegetation; see *Recommended Campsite* diagram page 81).
- Place your tent, if possible, with the open end close to some trees so you will have quick and easy access to them if necessary.
- Your sleeping location should not be on or near any type of trail.
- Do not sleep in the open (under the stars, without a tent).
- Do not sleep in a tent or other shelter used for cooking.
- Keep your sleeping area free of food odors; this is

AERIAL VIEW OF CAMPSITE

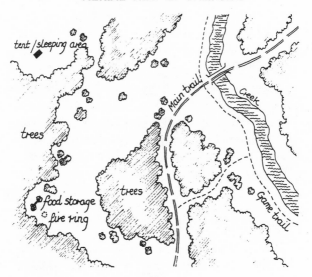

Aerial View of Campsite
(Courtesy Yellowstone National Park)

essential in reducing the likelihood of a bear entering your tent.

- Before retiring, check to be certain there are no food items (snacks, gum) remaining in your tent, pockets, pack, and so on.
- Wash thoroughly before retiring; the removal of food odors from your hands and face is important.
- Do not sleep in the same clothes in which you cooked.
- Sleep with a flashlight within easy reach.

Cooking

Lodging Area

Cabins and lodges may have picnic tables available for guests. If you are cooking or eating at these facilities, use the precautions described above under *Roadside and Picnic Areas*. Portable grills, hibachis, and so on, along with their associated food remnants and odors, are also attractants and should be appropriately stored away from bears.

R.V. and Trailer Parking

- Ventilate your camper or trailer unit well to minimize food preparation odors.
- See the instructions for *Tent Camping* below.

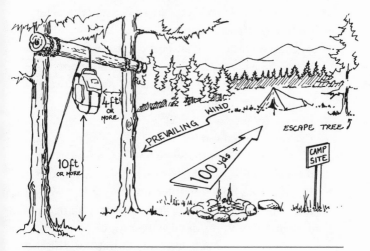

Recommended Campsight
(Courtesy Yellowstone National Park)

The Campground

- Cook with a liquid petroleum or gasoline stove instead of a campfire; this reduces and confines odors, scraps, and food droppings that are attractants.
- Avoid cooking odorous foods like bacon and fish.
- Do not cook or prepare food in any manner in your tent, regardless of the weather. Place your cooking shelter, if you have one, as far from your tent as possible — depending on the configuration and layout of the campground (one hundred yards is recommended in backcountry campsites).
- Use cooking shelters where provided.
- Always cook one hundred yards away from sleeping area, even if you are only preparing a late night cup of hot chocolate.
- In coastal areas, cook and eat on the beach below high tide where any odors and food remnants will be eliminated by the next tidal change (be aware of local requirements).
- Do not fry foods.
- Use freeze-dried foods.
- Do not cook more than you will eat; leftovers are difficult to dispose of or store, and are attractants.
- Wash dishes and cooking equipment immediately after eating and in your cooking area, not at streamsides or lakeshores.
- Be meticulously neat; even tiny crumbs on the

Grizzly bears in Yellowstone National Park.

Grizzly bears playing in water.

Black bear sow and three cubs on a snowbank in Yellowstone National Park.

©Gary Brown

(Courtesy Glacier National Park)

These three photos (top, bottom, and opposite page bottom) show that black bears can be various colors.

(Courtesy Yellowstone National Park)

Note the color similarity between the lightest of the black bears below and this grizzly bear.

(Courtesy Yellowstone National Park)

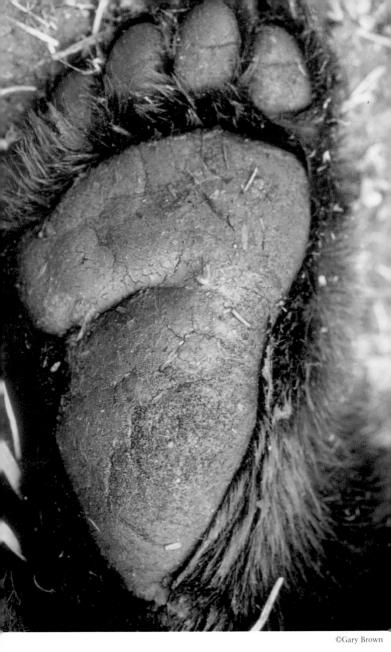

Grizzly bear hindpaw.

ground may attract bears, and in time their
accumulation becomes a major attractant.
- Clean up scrupulously after eating.

Food Storage

Lodging Area

Bears are attracted to foods in vehicles, which are bear
resistant, not bear proof. Food-conditioned bears have
gained entrance through open windows, by bending
doors and knocking out windows, and through soft-top
or -sided vehicles that offer no resistance.

- Remove all food items or other attractants, including
  ice chests, from your vehicle at night, or anytime
  vehicle is left unattended for more than an hour.
- Be certain all vehicle windows are *completely*
  closed; bears have entered open vehicle windows
  (or hooked their claws in partially open windows
  and removed them) and torn out back seats to
  gain entrance to a vehicle trunk.
- All food items, including pet and livestock food,
  should be removed from the backs of pickups.
- Place all attractants in your room (only if it's of
  solid construction) and close all windows when you
  leave; remember, tent-cabins are not bear resistant.
- Lodges in bear country often have secure areas
  where attractants may be stored.
- If you are unable to store attractants in your room

or at a lodge facility, secure them in the trunk of your car or cab of your truck.

- Do not feed bears; be no part of a situation where motel, lodge, or restaurant managers are baiting bears into the area for guests to view. This is not uncommon and results in increased opportunities for bear attacks and serious human injury.

The Campground

Foods, cooking utensils, garbage, and other attractants must be stored anytime they are not in use or being transported. Secure all food, beverages, and cooking and eating utensils, including stoves, grills, beverage (including water) containers, and water basins, by placing them in sealed plastic bags. Store other odorous items, such as toiletries, lotions, and insect repellents, in the same location as your food and utensils, as described below. Never leave foods unattended if they are not properly stored.

Ice chests or other types of coolers are wonderful for camping, but they are not bear resistant. Secure them, even if empty (they will contain food odors), and not just under your vehicle or trailer or in the back of your pickup but rather with the following secure storage methods.

R.V. AND TRAILER CAMPING

Store all of your attractants by one of these methods:

- In bear-resistant storage boxes/lockers, buildings, or caches, if they are provided in the campground (this is the preferred method).
- In your vehicle trunk, truck cab, R.V., or

camper/camping trailer (if constructed of nonpliable material); remember, soft-sided vehicles and camping units are not secure storage areas, and hard-sided units may be damaged by bears seeking attractants; be certain the windows of your vehicle are rolled up completely.

STORAGE METHODS FOR TENT CAMPING

Your foods, garbage, and other attractants must be stored—meticulously—anytime, day or night, when they are not in use. If the campground provides facilities (food boxes, poles, lockers, etc.) in which to store your attractants, use them. If such facilities are unavailable, or you have more food and equipment than the facilities will accommodate, use one or more of the methods described below. Whichever method you use, follow these guidelines:

- Store beverages with your food.
- Store cooking utensils, including stoves and grills, with your food.
- Secure any clothing you have used while cooking in the same manner as your food.
- Hanging food over a campfire in hopes that the smoke will mask the odors does not work; nor does submerging food in the water of a stream or lake.
- Do not take food items into your tent, even temporarily.
- Bags used for food storage must be used only for this purpose, and not for your sleeping bag or articles of clothing.
- Use extreme caution when you approach the area

where your food is stored.

- If your packs are not hung, place them on the ground outside your tent, empty and with the zippers and flaps opened to minimize any damage.

STORAGE IN PROVIDED FACILITIES AND SYSTEMS

- Some campsites provide bear-resistant storage facilities such as metal lockers, cages, elevated caches, fenced areas, buildings, barrels, or food boxes.
- When using these facilities, be certain the unit is appropriately latched or otherwise secured; remember, bears have been known to open latches and a variety of doors.
- Established vertical poles, or cables, wires, or poles suspended between uprights, are available in many campsites.
- Bear-resistant backpacker food storage canisters are available (by rental, loan, or purchase) from agencies and commercial outlets, and should be secured in the same manner as other containers; occasionally, depending on the nature of your campsite area and the management agency requirements, they may be placed on the ground in your food storage area, one hundred yards from your sleeping area.

PREPARATION FOR PROPER STORAGE

- Place attractants in sealed plastic bags.
- If you are hanging your attractants, you should then place the plastic bags in stuff bags, your pack,

bear-resistant backpacker food storage canisters, or
other sturdy containers that can be hanged.

HANGING ATTRACTANTS

- To raise the storage containers (pack, stuff bags,
  etc.), use the counterbalance system (see diagram
  on pages 90-91), or the method shown in the
  Recommended Campsite diagram (page 81).
- Check local requirements—some areas may
  require you to hang attractants at greater distances
  than 18 to 20 feet from the ground.
- Hanging food does not guarantee it will be safe;
  bears in some areas have learned to retrieve foods
  from lofty perches.
- Trees may be sparse at some campsites where
  hanging your food is necessary; if so, the extra walk
  to locate appropriate trees is well worth the effort.
- When camping above timberline (tree line), see
  the *Treeless Area Food Storage* diagram below.

STORAGE WITHOUT TREES OR OTHER FACILITIES

- Place your food and other attractants in airtight bags.
- Use bear-resistant food storage canisters (if
  available).
- Place your appropriately packaged attractants on
  the ground—in brush, if available—at least one
  hundred yards downwind from your sleeping area,
  and at least one hundred yards from your cooking
  area (the cooking area should also be at least one
  hundred yards from your sleeping area; see the

Treeless Area Food Storage diagram).

- Do not place attractants near trails or streams.
- Instead of placing attractants on the ground, you can hang the storage containers over a rock face (if available); you can also place them on the ground and pile boulders on them, adding your cooking pots to the top to sound a warning.

Camp and Area Sanitation

LODGING AREA

- Never leave garbage or trash outside of your cabin or other single-unit lodging facility.
- Dispose of all garbage and trash in provided bear-resistant receptacles.

THE CAMPGROUND

- Clean your campsite upon arrival, if necessary, and keep it clean thereafter; clean the fire pit, especially if you are not building a fire; if the fire pit contains garbage, food scraps, or trash, you may want to burn out the pit to reduce odors that may attract a bear.
- If there is a camp table, wash it upon your arrival and keep it clean.
- If careless campers with unsecured attractants are nearby, discuss the problem with them; if they are not willing to properly store attractants, move on.
- Wash your dishes in your cooking area, not along

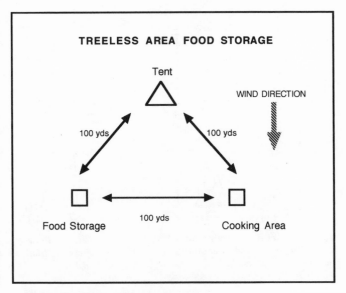

TREELESS AREA FOOD STORAGE

Treeless Area Food Storage
(© Patricia Brown)

streams, lake- or pondshore, or at faucets or other water supplies.

- Do not put out bird feeders; they often attract bears.

WASTEWATER

- Dispose of your wastewater (dishwater or excess cooking water) in a provided campground disposal sink. If a disposal sink is unavailable:
- Remove all food particles from the wastewater and treat these solids as garbage (see above).
- If a very hot open fire is available, pour the

1. *Locate a tree with a live sturdy branch; separate your food and other attractants into two bags of equal weight.*

2. *Throw rope (from tree trunk—so b reach.*

4. *Attach your second bag as high on the rope as you can reach and place the excess rope on top of the bag; provide a loop of rope near the bag for retrieval.*

5. *Push bag up wit to the level of other b*

ranch—at least 8'
nds are in your

3. *Be certain there are no rocks or other objects that a bear could stand on to reach your bags; attach one bag to rope end and raise completely to the branch.*

ong stick to raise it

6. *To retrieve bags, hook long stick in the loop near one bag. Other bag will follow.*

Counterbalance System of Food Storage

wastewater in the corner of the fire pit to allow drying and evaporation; occasionally stir and push the fire and hot coals into the wet area.

- If an open fire is unavailable, check bulletin boards or with campground attendants for other prescribed disposal methods; as a last resort, disperse the liquids on the ground at least one hundred yards from sleeping and cooking areas.

GARBAGE

- Dispose of your solid garbage and trash in the appropriate receptacle; if the campground does not have bear-resistant garbage cans or dumpsters, secure your garbage in the same manner as your food, and deposit it later in an appropriate receptacle.
- Do not place garbage or trash in outhouses.
- Do not bury or burn garbage or trash; neither is an efficient means of eliminating odors.
- Double bag and secure garbage and trash with your foods and carry it out of the backcountry.

LATRINE

- If camping in the backcountry, select a latrine area away from your sleeping and food storage locations, but not so far away that you will have to "hike in the wilderness" to find it, especially at night.
- Do not dispose of garbage or trash in any latrine area—for the obvious reason that you will not want to share that location with bears.

Personal Cleanliness

- While camping, keep as clean as possible.
- Wash up well after cooking or eating and before retiring.
- Do not sleep in the same clothing in which you cooked or ate; secure these clothes as you do your food.
- Some authorities believe the odors associated with sexual activity may attract bears.

Travel In and About Camps and Lodging Areas

Remember, you are in bear country, and bears may be in and around your lodging area or campground. Do not surprise a bear. Be alert and use caution when moving about between the specific areas (sleeping, cooking, latrine, rest room, food storage, parking, etc.) of your lodging facility or campground, especially at night.

- Make noise—talk, whistle—as you walk through the area.
- Use a flashlight when moving about in the dark.
- *Walk-in* campsites require some additional precautions: Do not leave your food and other attractants unattended while they are shuttled between the campsite and your vehicle or storage site; use extra caution when moving between your vehicle and campsite at night.

Activities Away from Camps and Lodging Areas

If you engage in the variety of activities often associated with bear country, those that take you away from your lodging or camp area, use the bear encounter avoidance measures specific to your activities in the following sections: 1. bicycling 2. boating 3. fishing 4. jogging, etc. (See pages 104-118).

If you are hiking near lodging areas, do not relax your precautions. Bears' day beds have been found within forty yards of a lodge area.

If you are traveling to a *backcountry wilderness lodge, cabin, or chalet,* use the avoidance measures outlined for your specific activities.

If you leave your campsite for the day, or even for a short trip, be certain to secure your food and other attractants.

Breaking Camp

- Be certain you have enough time at your departure to leave a clean camp.
- Clean your campsite thoroughly.
- If a bear has scattered food or garbage—yours or that of another camp—clean it up.
- Remember, pack out everything you packed in, including your garbage and trash; any attractants left behind may bring a bear into the camp and result in a tragic situation for the next campers.

- Do not forget to gather food and other items you have secured.

The Trailhead

Arrival at a trailhead is a critical period during a backpacking trip—the moment you ask yourself, "Do I have everything?" Besides food, tent, fishing equipment, and so on, do you have the items necessary to secure attractants from bears, including rope, bags, and/or a bear-resistant food canister?

There is the potential to encounter a bear at the trailhead. Be alert, and use the avoidance measures outlined under the *Roadside and Picnic Areas* (pages 72-73). Read the trailhead signs and bulletin boards.

Parking and Food Security

Park your vehicle legally. You should not store any food or item that would be an attractant for bears in the vehicle. However, if you must leave items in the vehicle, try to park where the vehicle will be in the shade as much as possible. Attractants in a cool vehicle do not emit as much odor as those heated in an ovenlike vehicle in the sun.

Place all attractants in your vehicle trunk, in the cab of your pickup, or in a secure area of your hard-sided recreational vehicle, and out of sight if possible. Again, hard-sided top racks are not bear resistant. Be certain all vehicle windows are completely closed.

Camping

Camping is normally not permitted at trailheads. If it is allowed, however, the avoidance measures applicable to sleeping, cooking, food storage, area sanitation, personal cleanliness, travel in and about camp, and breaking camp apply. See the sections on *The Campground* under these categories (pages 74-95) for the necessary guidelines. Some remote trailheads where camping is permitted do not have garbage facilities. You will need to secure and later dispose of your garbage at the nearest appropriate garbage can. *Never place garbage or trash in an outhouse or other toilet facility*

Shuttles

Often hikers begin and end their trips at different trailheads. When this is the case, be certain that you do not leave your equipment (attractants) unattended and unsecured during a shuttle, even for "just a few minutes." Hikers have returned to pick up their equipment and found it shredded, scattered, and sometimes completely gone.

Security of Property

Sadly, bears are not the only vandals you need to protect your property against. Vehicles are broken into and contents stolen by two-legged animals (car clouters) while unattended at trailheads. Lock your vehicle, after securing everything out of sight, and if possible leave nothing of value behind.

On the Trail
(Overnight or Day Trips)

Finally, you have broken away from the rigors and pressures of civilization, developments, crowds, traffic, and your vehicle, and are experiencing freedom in the wild. Backpackers normally experience more wonderful views of landscape and wildlife while on the trail than at their destination. However, you also are entering bear country where surprise encounters often occur, and where avoidance measures are more exacting and difficult. You are vulnerable to bears that use the same trails you do. The term "trail" here includes both wildlife and human trails (maintained or otherwise), as well as off-trail cross-country travel.

Alertness

Alertness is paramount while hiking, regardless of your route, whether on an established trail or traveling cross-country. Too often people hike with their heads down, more concerned with where they place their feet than with what is around them. Obviously, where you place your boots is important: you do not want to stumble, twist an ankle, or fall, and the trail is also where you may see bear sign. However, when you are not looking up and about you, you cannot be alert and aware of your surroundings, nor identify bears, some bear sign, or climbable trees. Try to balance your awareness between the trail and the country through which you are hiking—your total environment.

Surprise

The potential to surprise a bear along the trail is considerable. Bears use human trails to move from area to area. They prefer trails that are located in valley bottoms and along streams and lakeshores—areas with the good soils and moisture that produce excellent vegetation and other bear foods. Any trail where travel is easy for people is also preferred by bears, and therefore such places commonly bring the two species together. But hikers often encounter bears off-trail, too, so remain vigilant wherever you are.

In many areas, bears are more active at night, thus you should hike only during daylight hours. You will be less likely to encounter a bear, and your visibility will be better.

There is safety in hiking in a group. Hike at a pace comfortable for everyone in your group, with no one rushing ahead and no stragglers. A pace that is too fast may not only fatigue the slower members of the group but also decrease the amount of time an alerted bear has to avoid an encounter.

Design your route to prevent surprising a bear, hiking as much as possible in the open so bears may be detected. The topography and vegetation of many areas do not allow this, but keep it in mind, and give it a try.

Noise is your primary method of preventing surprise. Traveling in a group, or at least with a partner, provides the most natural and simple kind of noise—conversation. Talk about anything—just make noise. If you are alone or if conversation with others is difficult, sing, talk to yourself or the bears ("Hey bear, I'm a friend, don't be afraid, go away, just leave me alone!"), shout, bang pots, or wear bells on your pack or attached to your bootlaces (although some bear authorities believe that the louder the noise the better, and that bells are not loud enough). A pebble-filled can attached to your pack is an efficient noisemaker.

Noise becomes even more important when visibility is restricted by dense vegetation, bends in the trail, large boulders, logs, fog, or rain.

In dense forests, where sound carries poorly and sight distance is limited, increase both your noise and your caution. A strong wind in your face means a bear has less chance to detect you by sound and smell; you should thus increase your noise.

Bears may not only be around a corner, but feeding just off the trail. Use extreme caution when visibility is poor in any direction. Remember, there are some limitations to noise—other sounds or elements may mask the sound of your approach. Be alert!

Binoculars

Binoculars are handy items to have with you. Besides enhancing your overall viewing, they will afford you the opportunity to identify "the dark, bearlike object" in the meadow ahead, to inspect bear sign from a distance, and to better see the areas you are approaching. They may add weight to your travel gear, but they add considerably to your enjoyment and safety.

Bear Sign

Be on the lookout for bear sign—evidence that a bear is or has been in the area. If you observe what you believe is bear sign, heighten your awareness. Identify the sign: Has there been bear activity here? If so, you may wish to make a detour from your route, or even leave the area. *Use extreme caution!* Be alert, have good sight-distance, and make noise.

Trail Stops

Stopping along the trail to eat, view the landscape, or just rest is common among hikers but also a time when they may become more vulnerable to the curiosity and aggressiveness of habituated and food-conditioned bears. Be cautious and keep the following pointers in mind:

- Never stop in an area where there is bear sign.
- Select a location that has good visibility in all

directions, so you are able to spot an approaching bear early on.

- The group should sit where individuals are able to see in each direction.
- If you are eating, keep your pack, supplies, and food consolidated, so there are fewer attractants out and you can pack up quickly and easily.
- Be careful not to drop food or spill drinks on the ground, which would leave attractants that may lead a bear to the next people who travel along the trail. Repack any trash and garbage and take it out with you.
- If a bear approaches, quickly pack up and move away (see Chapter 4, *Encounters with Bears*).

Side Trips

Side trips off the trail or primary route can be exciting and fun adventures. They may serve a variety of purposes, including better viewing, seeking a specific feature, or sometimes only a toilet stop. Before leaving the trail for a side trip, remember:

- Do not leave your pack along the trail—or anywhere—unattended or unprotected from bears.
- If you intend a lengthy side trip and wish to be unencumbered by your pack, move well off the trail and secure everything in the same manner you would in a backcountry campsite (see *Food Storage*, pages 83-88); be certain to note some

landmarks so you are able to locate your gear
when you return.
- *Stop and eat before you arrive at your destination
campsite*, if at all possible. This will leave the odors
of cooking, eating, and dishwashing well away
from your camping and sleeping sites. Use the
methods outlined in *Cooking* and *Food Storage—
The Campground* (pages 81-88).

OTHER ACTIVITIES IN BEAR COUNTRY

Observing and Photographing Bears

Some of the more serious encounters with bears have
occurred when people were attempting to observe or
photograph them at close range. So if you want to take
pictures of bears, do so from a safe distance.

First, find out from local area wildlife offices,
information centers, or other agency offices where and
how to best view bears, specific viewing areas, and the
best times of day for observation.

View and photograph bears from at least one
hundred yards (less than that *is* a risk, and more than
one hundred yards *may still be a risk*), preferably with
binoculars and long lenses. Photographers should use at
least a 400mm lens, and those people with point-and-
shoot cameras will have to be satisfied with showing

Bear Feeding Along Side of Trail
(© Gary Brown)

friends at home the beautiful, broad landscape shot with "that small dark object in the center."

Do not approach or crowd bears. Allow them to continue their natural activities—to be themselves. If you observe a change in a bear's behavior—moving closer or farther away from you, swinging its head from side to side, pawing at the ground, raising its hackles (hairs on back of the neck), ceasing to feed or rest, or making sounds—you are too close, regardless of the distance. Immediately back away and leave the area. Some attacks have occurred not because the people continued to directly approach the bears, but because they did not retreat, and therefore remained a threat to the bears. If a bear you are observing begins moving away, do not pursue it!

Many people obsessed with getting a close view or photograph of a bear have been seriously mauled, and several have been killed.

Bicycle Travel and Camping

Bicycling, and mountain biking in particular, is becoming a more popular means by which to access and enjoy the backcountry (where permitted). However, there *are* a few additional concerns when bicycling in bear country.

Cyclists are particularly vulnerable in areas with "roadside" bears. Many bicyclists have had disturbing experiences with bears, including being chased or virtually pedaling into bears along trails and roads. To minimize the opportunities for bear encounters, take the precautionary measures outlined in this chapter that are applicable to your specific location and activities.

When camping, do not sleep in the open—use a tent or camper cabin. Foods and other attractants must be properly stored. Use the appropriate food storage measures for a drive-in or backpacker campground (see pages 83-88) and be certain you carefully check all bicycle panniers, packs, and saddlebags for remnants of lunch, snacks, gum, and other attractants.

Off-road bicycle travel is of particular concern. A mountain bike zooming downhill is moving at a high speed and is relatively quiet, providing a greater potential for a close encounter with a bear than does hiking. The cyclist also often rides in dense vegetation, creating blind corners. This, coupled with speed, allows the cyclist to easily surprise and crowd a bear.

As a cyclist in bear country, keep your head up, be alert to your surroundings, and travel at a speed that gives you time to observe and evaluate what is ahead of you. Attach a noisemaker to your bicycle. Some bicyclists use bells, a closed container filled with pebbles, or even a piece of cardboard attached to the wheel spokes and struck by their movement.

And remember, off-road use of bicycles is prohibited in many areas.

Motorcycle Travel

People traveling by motorcycle face the same basic problems and concerns in bear country as those in automobiles or pickup trucks—to appropriately store attractants, to avoid surprising or crowding a bear, and so on. However, there are a few additional considerations for the motorcyclist, similar to those encountered by the person bicycling.

To begin with, a motorcyclist—like a bicyclist—is exposed. Also, the motorcycle has no bear-resistant features such as trunks. (Even hard saddlebags, storage boxes, and trailers quickly yield to a bear's teeth and claws.) This necessitates removing all attractants from the motorcycle during stops and securing them in a lodge, in a motel, in a campground-provided storage facility, or, if tent camping, by hanging.

As a motorcyclist traveling in bear country, refer to *Bicycle Travel and Camping* (pages 104-105), and the other segments that apply to your specific activities.

Water Travel and Camping

Water travel—by boat, canoe, kayak, raft, or other watercraft—is an exciting activity and a wonderful means of moving through the backcountry, *especially bear country*. There is considerably less potential for a bear encounter when you are traveling on the water. And, you are in a excellent position for observing wildlife, including bears, along the shorelines. However, there are some special bear concerns when traveling by water.

Water and Boating Safety

- Water is a powerful and unpredictable force, and water travel requires appropriate knowledge and skills. Always travel with an experienced boater.

Launch Areas

- Vehicle parking measures are basically the same as if you were at *The Trailhead* (page 95-97).
- Do not leave attractants unattended during shuttles, even those trips between your vehicle and watercraft, if the distance is any more than a few feet.

- Boats left at developed dock facilities are susceptible to bears boarding in search of foods; keep a clean boat and remove all attractants when it is unattended.

Traveling

- Most watercraft allow you to carry more foods—including odorous items—than when backpacking, or bicycling; this means extra attention to food storage is required.
- Rest stops and lunch breaks are on shorelines, which are travel routes for bears; use caution and refer to the measures outlined in *Roadside and Picnic Areas* (page 72-73).
- Do not approach or crowd bears along the shorelines; even though you may feel secure in your watercraft, you are vulnerable to a charging bear which is powerful and capable of moving very quickly in shallow water; and remember, bears are excellent swimmers.
- During portages, use the measures outlined in *On the Trail, Side Trips* (pages 97-102); and do not leave food or other attractants unattended, which means you will need to hang some items if there are only two in the group and more attractants than each person can carry in a single portage.

Campsites

- Select a campsite well away from the water, since shorelines of streams, lakes, and ponds frequently serve as bear travel routes.

- Islands do not make ideal campsites; bears commonly visit or inhabit these retreats.
- Do not camp at the mouths of spawning streams; this is where fish often congregate, and they may be readily sought by bears.
- Utilize the measures outlined in *Travel in Bear Country—The Campground* (pages 74-80).

Food Storage

- Store foods and other attractants as outlined in *Food Storage—The Campground* (page 83-88).
- Submerging foods does not work; bears readily locate attractants under water.
- Storing foods in your watercraft, even if moored well away from shore, is a *bad idea*; bears smell and swim well, and some unhappy campers have found themselves in dire straits when their canoe, kayak, boat, or raft was destroyed by a bear retrieving their food; be certain there are no attractants left in your watercraft.
- Odors of attractants often linger in watercraft so keep the craft as clean as possible.
- You may wish to attach bells or other noisemakers to your craft as an early warning measure.

Fishing

- Utilize the measures outlined in *Fishing* (page 113-115).
- If you fish from your canoe, kayak, boat, or raft,

you have the additional problem of getting fish odors on and in the watercraft; this requires and extra-careful cleanup.

Horse and Other Stock Travel

Backcountry travel with horses and mules is quite common in some bear country, and people who use these animals have few bear encounters. Horses and mules are used for riding and to carry (pack) equipment and supplies. Donkeys, llamas, and goats are also used to pack in some areas. Bears appear to easily detect stock, associate the animals with people, and, for the most part, keep their distance.

The methods used by stock parties to minimize the potential for an encounter with a bear are essentially the same as those the backpacker uses, but a few additional measures specifically relate to stock:

- Be certain to follow the requirements for stock use as outlined by the responsible managing agencies.
- Treat stock feed (pellets, grain) as you would human food and other attractants, using appropriate storage measures.
- Do not pack large food containers, such as ice chests, unless you are prepared to hang them.
- You will have additional food security concerns at the trailhead if you are carrying stock feed in your trailer, truck, or other vehicle, including any remnants in the manger or feed bags; bears have

seriously damaged horse trailers seeking these foods.

- Feed your stock well away from your sleeping area.
- If you overnight with your stock at a lodging area or campground, use the appropriate measures outlined in this chapter.

Dogs in Bear Country

Dogs readily disturb and excite bears and are a cause of encounters. Whether a pet or a hunting dog, it may conflict with a bear by chasing or barking, soliciting a reaction from the bear. If the dog is not initially killed, it often retreats to its master, bringing along its newfound, irritated "companion." Several people have been seriously mauled as a result of this scenario. Bears also have destroyed dogs and then, continuing to feel threatened, attacked the dogs' owners.

Dogs barking at roadside bears from vehicle windows have been known to aggravate the bears to a point that major conflicts have occurred with the vehicles' occupants as well as everyone nearby.

Dogs should definitely not be in the backcountry. If your "best friend" is with you elsewhere in bear country, you must maintain control of it at all times, which normally means on a leash. Remember also that dog food is an attractant, like any other food. Store it, along with dog bowls, in the same manner as you do your food.

Winter Travel and Camping

Do not discount the potential of a bear encounter during the winter. Some bears in the southern and southeastern areas of the United States, where adequate foods are available year-round, may den for only a short period or not at all. In areas where bears hibernate throughout the winter, a bear may leave its den during a period of warm weather, though it usually remains close to its retreat. No matter what the season, avoid known denning areas. Hibernating bears are easily awakened and may be dangerous when disturbed.

Do not ignore safe travel measures just because there is snow on the ground. In late winter and early spring bears begin to emerge from their dens and move about in search of nourishment. Minimizing the potential of an encounter while traveling and camping in bear country during these seasons requires the previously outlined precautions for hiking and camping, as well as a few additional efforts.

As bears begin to travel again after hibernation, they often use the routes of least resistance—ski trails and snowshoe tracks, hiking trails (even those covered in snow), frozen streams, snow-machine and four-wheeler tracks, and conventional vehicle roads.

Appropriate campsites are more difficult to establish in snow country, and there is an inherent awkwardness in having to don your skis or snowshoes to travel between each campsite area. But bears do not experience such difficulties and will seek attractants where they exist. You should therefore separate your sleeping area from your cooking and food storage areas in winter as you would at other times—by at least one hundred yards.

As always, *do not prepare, cook, or eat food in your tent.* Winter may introduce inclement weather into your trip, and cooking out in the rain and snow can be terribly uncomfortable. The use of a tarp or other covering as a cooking shelter should facilitate your food preparation and eating efforts.

Campfires are often constructed during the winter for warmth, as well as for drying clothes and equipment, and you may also be tempted to burn your garbage and trash. However, wintertime fires often do not burn well, especially during storms, due to excess moisture in the wood. The combustion of a winter fire is normally inadequate to completely eliminate the attracting odors of your garbage and trash. Treat garbage the same as you would during the summer: Secure it and pack it out.

Food storage is more difficult when you are standing in a few feet of snow, especially while on skis or snowshoes. Exercise patience and perserverence. Remember, the bottom of the storage bag (pack) must be at least ten feet from the surface below it—the top of the snow, not the ground two feet below the snow.

If you are camping above timberline, place your food in a snowbank well away from camp.

Fishing

Fishing often brings people into bear country, more specifically directly into good bear habitat. There are endless opportunities for a person fishing to encounter a bear. Remember, bears feed on vegetation in riparian areas along streams and the shores of lakes and ponds, and they also fish, usually where an abundance of fish—a spawn—makes the effort worthwhile. At a stream active with heavy spawning, there may be a congregation of bears, or a single bear seeking a lone fish in shallow water. Other animals often die along shorelines and their carcasses attract bears. These locations are also excellent travel routes for bears.

Surprising a bear may be harder to avoid along a stream or lake as visibility is often limited by the dense vegetation, and the sound of your approach is masked by the noise of moving water—the current of a stream or the wave action of a lake. Also, people fishing are notoriously quiet—silently sneaking up on the water, deep in thought, contemplating the appropriate bait, lure, or fly and the moment of the strike. Encounters between bears and people fishing are not uncommon.

Always fish with a partner—never fish alone. As you travel to your fishing hole, use the measures described in *On the Trail* to minimize your chances of an encounter with a bear.

Be alert! Along streams or lakes, bear sign may include tracks, heavily worn trails, and fish remnants—heads, tails, intestines, eggs, and sometimes a whole fish that the bear will return to shortly. Scavenging birds along a stream may also indicate that bears have been feeding. Make noise often to alert bears and provide them the opportunity to move away.

In some locations, a few habituated and food-conditioned bears have learned to compete for the "catch." They will approach in hopes that you will drop your fish for their taking. If accosted, promptly drop the fish and leave the area.

If you keep fish (that is, if you do not release them back into the stream or lake), clean them along the stream or lake, not near or in camp or back at the lodge. (An exception might be made if there is a convenient fish-cleaning station at the lodge or dock facility.) Dispose of the entrails from a point at least one hundred yards along the shore from any camp. Puncture the fish's air bladder to prevent it from floating, and throw the viscera into deep water well out into the stream or lake so it will not wash up on the shore. Keep your catch in tightly sealed plastic bags.

Cooking fish is extremely odorous. I strongly recommend that you not keep or cook fish in a backcountry camp. If you do choose to do so, you must treat all remains of the fish as any other garbage—secure them and haul them out of the backcountry.

Handling fish, especially cleaning them, results in fish odors accumulating on you and your clothing. Wash your hands well after handling the fish, and do not sleep in these clothes. Secure the clothes as you would your food and other attractants.

Practice good prevention measures and enjoy your fishing.

Hunting

Many species of game animals are hunted in North American bear country, and hunters have had serious conflicts with bears. Hunting, including the pursuit of bears, involves some actions that are quite contrary to the prescribed methods for preventing encounters.

The nature of much hunting activity is moving silently and secretively through a variety of vegetation, including dense foliage, which greatly enhances your likelihood of surprising and crowding a bear, including a sow with cubs.

Also, successful hunters possess animal carcasses— small game birds, squirrels, or large animals (elk, moose, deer, and bear)—that are highly attractive to bears. The bird and small-game hunter is normally able to properly secure the kill, but the big-game hunter is faced with handling a large carcass, which requires considerable effort and time. The amount of attracting odor is increased with the size of the carcass, as is the quantity of blood. And often much of this blood is on the hunters and their clothing.

Bears are attracted to carcasses not only in the field, but in the backs of pickups, in trailers, and wherever they may be hanging or temporarily stored.

Big-game hunters leave "gut piles," which are high in protein and quite attractive to bears. Many hunters have had close encounters when they have intruded upon a bear defending a gut pile that they or other hunters created.

As a hunter, use the measures outlined in the applicable travel and camping segments to minimize encounters with bears. Here are a few additional precautions that you should practice:

- Know and abide by all applicable hunting regulations; honor and practice good hunting ethics.
- Be alert and always have good visibility ahead of you (this is especially critical if you are pursuing a wounded bear); make every effort to prevent surprising a bear at close range.
- Remember that hunting with dogs (other than bear-hunting dogs) may create further problems. See *Dogs in Bear Country* in this chapter (page 110).
- Remove the carcass from the area as soon as possible.
- If you must leave the carcass for any length of time, hang it where you can see it from a distance; when you return, use binoculars to observe the area around the carcass; approach from upwind, making noise; use extreme caution if the carcass has been disturbed; if a bear has claimed the carcass, concede—the bear wins.
- Do not leave a gut pile or carcass on or near a

trail or road.
- Avoid gut piles you happen to come upon.
- Do not take a carcass into your camp. Hang or otherwise secure it at least one hundred yards from your camp. Some agencies provide you with poles or other means to secure game, but if you hang a carcass, it should be at least ten feet above the ground and six feet from any vertical support.

Jogging

Jogging in bear country is much like hiking. While jogging you are somewhat preoccupied (especially due to your faster pace) with placing your feet in the appropriate spots, and are not as alert to your surroundings as you would be if walking. And, as in bicycling, you are traveling at a relatively fast rate—capable of rapidly moving into a bear's space and crowding it. Depending on your personal conditioning, you may be breathing in such a manner as to be incapable of making the noise necessary to warn a bear of your presence. Also, joggers often run in the early morning or late evening when bears are more active. All or any of the above may contribute to an encroachment into a bear's critical space, and a resulting serious encounter.

Many a jogger, the author included, has found him- or herself in this situation. Tragically, some cases have resulted in serious maulings.

- Jog elsewhere if bears are known to be presently using an area.
- Jog with a companion, and talk or make noise.
- Be alert to your surroundings; look for bear sign.
- Remember, you are moving at a pace faster than a walk, and you can be upon a bear before it has the opportunity to detect you.
- Be extra-cautious in dense vegetation, or anywhere visibility is limited.
- Refer to the *On the Trail* segment of this chapter.

WOMEN IN BEAR COUNTRY

DURING THE PAST TWO DECADES, theories have been advanced that there exists a correlation between menstruation and bear attacks. Some agency managers and others have strongly recommended that women do not travel in the backcountry during their menstrual periods.

However, the evidence that bears are attracted to menstrual odors more than other attractants is not conclusive, nor is there statistical evidence to link menstruation with recorded bear attacks. The current general opinion of bear managers, researchers, and other authorities is that women should not be discouraged from traveling in bear country during their menstrual periods, but should practice some very specific precautionary measures:

- Keep yourself as clean and odor-free as possible; though menstrual odors may not cause bear attacks, they may—like other odors—attract a bear into close contact.
- Use premoistened, unscented cleaning towelettes.
- Use tampons instead of pads.
- Wrap all used tampons in aluminum foil, place in a zipper lock or Ziploc plastic bag, and store as you would garbage, foods, and other attractants.
- Do not place tampons or towelettes in a latrine, or bury them.
- Burning tampons or pads completely requires an extremely hot fire and considerable time; any remnant in the fire pit is an attractant for bears.
- Use good judgement; if you are uncomfortable traveling in bear country during your period, consider adjusting the timing of the trip.

Remember, cosmetics, perfumes, and other scented items are also attractants and should not be brought along. Bring only toiletry items that are unscented.

4

Encounters with Bears (Your Actions and Reactions)

There are many types of encounters with bears, ranging from a distant observation to a close confrontation—an attack. Most confrontations resolve themselves with the bears fleeing in one direction and the people retreating in another. How you fare in an encounter with a bear will depend on your knowledge of bears and their habitat, on your alertness, and on the actions you take as you travel through bear country.

Though many people believe the grizzly bear to be the more dangerous of the two species you might encounter, black bears also are capable of attacking, and can cause serious mental trauma, bodily injury, and even death. Never discount a black bear's power, quickness, and ability to inflict harm.

Some of your behavior during an encounter should depend upon the species of bear and the individual bear's actions. Know how to interpret the bear's "body

121

language"—posturing. The bear's awareness of you, and its actions, should dictate your response.

Good knowledge, preplanning, and calm, calculated actions will give you some control over the outcome of an encounter. Everyone in your travel group must understand the appropriate actions necessary during an encounter, since one panicky person can jeopardize the entire party. Before traveling, go over possible scenarios with the group. Discuss the appropriate responses to various kinds of encounters.

Each encounter or confrontation will be unique, but described below are general situations your group might find itself facing.

BEAR OBSERVED IN THE DISTANCE— *NOT* AWARE OF YOU

You should:

- Not make abrupt moves or noises that would startle it and alert it to your presence (if you have not made adequate noise to alert it by the time you spot it, then let well enough alone).
- Move away; give it plenty of space, allowing it to move on or pass through—provide it a "way out."
- If it is a sow with cubs, turn back and leave the area; alter your plans; hike elsewhere.
- If it is not a sow with cubs, and you decide to continue, detour widely (hundreds of yards, not

just out of its sight), downwind, around the bear;
be aware of its direction of travel so you do not
meet again.
- If a detour is not possible, wait for the bear
to leave, or, again, turn back and hike elsewhere.
- *If you are doubtful about detouring to any degree, turn
back—retreat!*

BEAR OBSERVED IN THE DISTANCE— AWARE OF YOU

If the Bear Flees

You should:

- Not approach or pursue the bear.
- Detour widely around the bear.
- Attempt to remain on a route that provides a long
sight-distance and is upwind from the bear's route.
- Attempt to keep the bear in sight so that if the
bear's and your travel routes begin to intersect,
you may avoid the bear.
- Turn back if there is any possibility the bear will
be on your travel route.

If the Bear Stands on Its Hind Legs to Better Identify You

(This improves its scent and view of you; its head
may turn from side to side while bipedal; this is not an
aggressive posture.)

You should:

- Remain calm.
- Not approach the bear.
- Allow the bear to determine what you are by waving your arms and talking to it in a normal, firm, monotone voice.
- Not make loud noises or abrupt movements that could startle or threaten the bear and provoke an attack.
- Not run.
- Look for a climbable tree (see *Climbing a Tree To Escape a Bear* on pages 133-134).

If the Bear Remains in Its Location

The bear may continue standing, or return to its previous activity of feeding, traveling, etc.)

You should:

- Move away from the bear.
- Consider a very wide detour around the bear, if possible— against, hundreds of yards, not just out of its sight; and, if possible, remain aware of the bear's location.
- Remain upwind so the bear has your scent.
- If a detour is not possible, *turn back and hike elsewhere.*

If the Bear Runs Toward You

(It may only be approaching for better identification.)

You should:

- Remain calm.
- Not make abrupt movements or loud noises that might threaten the bear and provoke an attack.
- Not run.
- Allow the bear to determine what you are by slowly waving your arms and talking to it in a normal, firm, monotone voice.
- Look for a climbable tree and, if possible, drop an item of diversion and climb (see *Climbing a Tree To Escape a Bear* on pages 133-134).
- If you are in a developed area, seek safety in a vehicle or building.

A SOW WITH CUBS

IF YOU OBSERVE CUBS, or a sow with cubs, silently and cautiously retreat—leave the area—immediately! Remember, cubs are not the little playful bundles of fur we associate with the word "cub," but may weigh more than 100 pounds (150 pounds for grizzly bears). Even if a cub appears to be alone, be assured the mother is close by. Do not approach. As you retreat, remain aware of the bears' location and activities.

Grizzly Bear Sow with Three Cubs
(Courtesy Yellowstone National Park)

If a sow with cubs observes you, react according to the situation and recommendations under *The Close Encounter—A Confrontation* (below). Also, react as if it were a close encounter if you observe what might be a bear protecting carrion.

A BOLD BLACK BEAR

A BEAR MAY BOLDLY WALK into an area in an attempt to obtain foods—enter a tent, break into a cabin or vehicle, or even attempt to take food from you along the trail—this is obviously a food-conditioned, habituated bear. Often, but not always, a black bear may be chased away. You may be able to dissuade a black bear if your aggressive actions overcome its desire to obtain your food. (Do not attempt aggression if it is a grizzly bear or a sow with cubs, or if you have any doubt as to the species.)

You should:

- Keep a safe distance and use good judgement.
- Be mildly aggressive to attempt to chase off the bear (though not a sow with cubs).
- Yell, blow a whistle, bang cooking gear, throw rocks or other objects.
- Not provide the bear with food or any other reward.
- Not attempt to retrieve food if the bear is successful in obtaining any.
- If the bear is persistent and will not leave within approximately a minute, climb a tree (see *Climbing a Tree To Escape a Bear* on pages 133-134), or leave the area.

THE CLOSE ENCOUNTER— A CONFRONTATION

A CLOSE ENCOUNTER may be initiated by the situations described above, or by suddenly finding yourself and a bear at close range. A surprise encounter often, and quickly, results in a charge.

If the Bear Closely Approaches and Stands on its Hind Legs

(It may identify you, not display aggression, and leave; it may look toward you—its head may turn from side to side—*continuing to have a better look to identify you.*)

You should:

- Remain calm; do not panic (quick alarming movements may also cause the bear to panic).
- *Not run* (you cannot outrun a bear, and running may incite the bear to chase and attack).
- Not make abrupt movements or loud noises that might threaten the bear and provoke an attack.
- Talk to the bear in a normal, firm, monotone voice.
- Back away; stop moving away if doing so appears to agitate the bear (if it clacks its teeth or jaws and/or makes moaning, woofing, or barking sounds).
- Seek safety in a vehicle or building or up a nearby tree if available; otherwise, leave the area.

If the Bear Approaches on All Four Legs

(This is an aggressive approach.)

The bear may:

- Swing its head from side to side (a display of nervousness and agitation).
- Present a side view of its body as if ignoring you (the bear is expressing dominance but is reluctant to charge—though it may still do so—and is seeking a way out of the situation).

- Look directly at you with its ears back (it is expressing a warning that it feels crowded and threatened).
- Further emphasize its distress with barking, woofing, or moaning sounds.
- Pop (clack) its jaws and teeth together, or give a series of woofs, or both (it is highly agitated and quite likely to charge).

You should:

- Not run; stay together as a group, and remain calm.
- Avoid direct eye contact with the bear.
- Talk to the bear in a normal, firm, monotone voice.
- Not imitate a bear's sounds, actions, or motions.
- Back away; give the bear space, a way out; attempt to reduce the bear's feeling of being crowded, even though it approached you; leave the area.
- Not turn your back on the bear; stop moving away if doing so agitates the bear (begin backing away again when the agitation ceases).
- Look for a climbable tree (see *Climbing a Tree To Escape a Bear* on pages 133-134).
- If it is a black bear, though not a sow with cubs, attempt to chase it off with mild aggression—yell, shout (not scream), below a whistle, throw rocks, bang camp gear. Do not respond this way if the bear is a grizzly.
- If you are able to back out of sight, keep moving and leave the area at a fast walk—do not run.

If the Bear Charges You—An Attack

- It may veer off or run by you or stop; *this is an attempt to scare you away.*
- It may leave after several bluff charges (some bears have learned that a bluff charge causes people to drop their packs with a resulting food reward; do not drop your pack).
- Though there may be no contact with you at this moment of the bear's aggression, there is a fine line between a bluff charge and actual contact with you.

You should:

- Remain calm; do not run.
- Attempt to reduce the bear's feeling of being threatened by not making aggressive movements or sounds.
- Avoid direct eye contact with the bear.
- Not yell, shout, or scream, but continue talking in a normal, firm, monotone voice.
- Not kick, strike, or lash out at the bear.
- Throw an object on the ground as a diversion (glove, jacket, hat, cup, sunglasses, camera—not food nor your pack) and *back away* from it; there is no safety in retreating into water (stream, lake)— bears like water and swim well.
- If the bear makes a bluff charge, *back away and leave the area*, or *climb a tree* after the bear stops or veers off (see *Climbing a Tree To Escape a Bear* on pages 133-134).
- If you are able to back out of sight, keep moving

and leave the area at a fast walk—do not run.

- If the aggressor is a black bear, though not a sow with cubs, attempt to chase it off with mild aggression—yell, shout (not scream), blow a whistle, throw rocks, bang camp gear; if the bear does not depart within approximately one minute, back away and climb a tree or leave the area.

Remember, in all situations, remain calm—do not panic. Panic, at best, results in a bear charging, and your falling from a tree, over logs, or off a cliff and breaking bones or suffering other trauma.

THE BEAR ATTACK

"Playing Dead"

In the event a bear attacks—makes physical contact with you—*play dead!* Typically, the bear's purpose is to remove a threat. Your objective is to protect your vital areas (abdominal and neck areas) and survive, while convincing the bear you are not a threat.

You should:

- Keep your pack on for protection (if you are wearing one).
- Drop to the ground with your legs up underneath your chest.
- Bend forward so your forehead touches your kneecaps.

- Protect your face with your forearms, by placing your arms close to your body with the elbows touching the outsides of your legs.
- Clasp your hands, interlocking the fingers, over the back of your neck.
- Do not struggle, attempt to fight, or attempt to physically restrain the bear—*remain motionless.*
- Do not cry out or make any noise—*remain silent.*
- If the bear swats you, roll with the blow, remaining in your cannonball position.
- Remain motionless and silent (for at least twenty minutes, though that may not be enough) to provide the bear time to leave.
- When you believe the bear is gone, cautiously peek, first moving only your eyelids and nothing else (a bear will often move off but continue to watch you, and any movement will renew the attack); listen; if you do not see or hear the bear, move only your head to look further about you; move slowly.
- Be patient—do not get up until you are certain the bear is gone; a bear may linger in the area for an hour.

Playing dead, remaining in the cannonball (fetal) position, and remaining silent when a bear is pawing and biting you will take a great measure of courage and discipline. But may be your only chance for survival. Practice quickly assuming the fetal position—you will have little time to think about it at the onset of an attack.

The Worst Case Scenario

If an attack persists—you believe the bear is not going to leave you, or it is dragging you from a tent, or out of your sleeping bag, preying upon you—attempt to get away. Be aggressive and defend yourself with everything available. Fight with your feet, fists, sticks, noise, rocks—whatever "weapons" are available. Strike, kick, gouge, bite—you are fighting for your life.

Here is where the value of a group may be most appreciated. The actions (noise, projectiles, aggressiveness, etc.) of other people may distract or chase off the bear, allowing you to reach safety.

Fighting has often turned away a black bear, and occasionally deterred a grizzly bear. This may seem bizarre and extreme, but if a bear will not cease attacking you, it may be your only, and final, chance.

CLIMBING A TREE TO ESCAPE A BEAR

TREE CLIMBING is a valid escape measure, *under certain circumstances*, but there are associated hazards.

- You must be able to reach a tree and safely climb to a position at which all of your body is at least ten feet off the ground before a charging bear also reaches the tree. (I am aware of four incidents where a person was seriously injured falling from a tree where they had sought safety; and of numerous cases of the person not reaching a safe height and being pulled from the tree by the bear.)

- The tree must have low, strong, climbable limbs.
- If you do climb a tree, remain in it for at least an hour to be certain the bear has departed the area; note its direction of travel, if possible.
- Once in a tree, do not decide to switch trees; people have been caught and mauled by a bear while changing trees.
- Upon coming down from your perch, leave the area immediately, and in a direction that will prevent another encounter with the bear.
- Remember, black bears and young grizzly bears climb trees quite well; adult grizzly bears have been known to "ladder up" trees that have available limbs; if a bear pursues you into the tree, aggressively fight as described in *The Worst Case Scenario*.

BEAR REPELLENTS

VARIOUS BEAR REPELLENTS have been tried for probably as long as humans have encountered bears, but none has proven a reliable means to deter bears.

Recently, some people have begun recommending the use of a small boat horn (pocket size) of the type usually used to scare off muggers, robbers, rapists, and capable of

Bear Repellent (Spray Canister)
(© Gary Brown)

damaging the hearing of any human. The reliability of this method as a bear repellent is uncertain.

A few promising chemical repellents in pressurized spray canisters have been developed and placed on the market during the last few years. The canisters are small and handheld, and discharge a irritant spray consisting of capsaicin, a derivative of cayenne peppers. Research indicates this repellent in most cases is effective in deterring bears.

However, do not allow carrying these canisters of spray repellent to give you a false sense of security. Your attitude and behavior while traveling in bear country should be the same as if you were empty-handed. Do not disregard the measures important in the prevention of encounters. Remember, the repellent *will not* prevent an encounter. It should be used as a last resort to avoid being mauled by a bear.

When you do require the repellent you must deploy it rapidly and properly. The canister must be readily accessible—in your hand or in a holster on your belt or pack shoulder strap, not in your pack or under your jacket. The repellent should be sprayed into a bear's face as it approaches and comes into range. The canister has a limited range—usually fifteen to twenty-four feet— and the spray is influenced by the wind. Also, the spray must reach the bear's eyes to be effective—a small target to hit in the time a bear requires to travel through the range.

A spray bear repellent may save you from serious injury and possibly death. But the best scenario is that you never reach the moment of truth—that you have used the measures to avoid encounters and prevent attacks in the first place.

IN CASE OF INJURY

IF SOMEONE IN YOUR TRAVEL GROUP becomes ill or is injured—whether by a bear, a bad fall, or other activity in the backcountry—be certain that during the haste to assist the person or seek aid you do not forget the necessary measures to prevent an encounter with a bear. More than one person seeking aid has hurriedly, but silently, traveled down a trail and surprised and crowded a bear at close range. Warn any aid parties of possible bear presence.

REPORTING OBSERVATIONS, ENCOUNTERS, AND ATTACKS

REPORT ALL BEAR OBSERVATIONS, encounters, property damage, and injuries to the appropriate authorities as soon as possible, regardless of the significance. The failure to do so may result in serious encounters for other bear country travelers.

5

Some Reminders— A Summary

Bear country generally includes places that people seek as retreats—locations to relax and spend free time, days off, or vacations. As you share this country with the black and grizzly bears during three of the four seasons (sometimes all seasons), remember that you are a visitor, a guest, and that your time here requires considerable planning and some specific personal behavior. This is the retreat of the most powerful animal on the North American continent, a symbol of wildness that must be understood, appreciated, and respected.

The responsibility of preventing encounters with bears is yours. You must understand the basic principles of safely using bear country—recognizing the causes of encounters, knowing how to avoid them (by planning, mental preparedness, traveling in a group, recognizing bear sign, averting surprise and crowding, securing attractants, and not feeding bears), and appropriately reacting in the face of a conflict.

The recommended avoidance measures outlined in this book have proven sound and effective. You may, however, find that local managing agencies require variations specific to their area, depending on its topography, its human traffic, and the learned behavior of its bear population. For example, the bears in the Sierra Nevada Mountains of California have learned to obtain what used to be considered well-secured food, therefore the parks and other agencies in that area have slightly different requirements for food security. In some areas of North America, the bears are more habituated to people, and precautionary measures more stringent.

Though there exist viable ways to avoid confrontations, and your chances of encountering a bear are statistically small, there is always a risk associated with sharing an environment with bears. Remember, there *is* no guarantee of your safety.

No one ever believes "it" will happen to them! But it does happen, and you increase the chances of it happening to you or someone near you by ignoring the measures recommended to minimize the chances of a bear encounter.

Study the guidelines within these pages for safe travel in bear country, and be able to effectively apply them without delay. *The Ten Basic Principles of Safe Travel in Bear Country* (pages 68-70) should become second nature to you.

The second most important element of traveling in bear country—the first being the prevention of an encounter—is to learn about bears and enjoy your outdoor adventure.

Danger--Entering Bear Country--A Risk

The backcountry you are entering is inhabited by black and grizzly bears. There are inherent dangers associated with hiking in bear country. You have come here voluntarily to experience this wilderness area. Please respect this wilderness and its inhabitants. THERE IS NO GUARANTEE OF YOUR SAFETY. Visitors have been injured and killed by bears. The chances of being attacked by a bear can be reduced by:

When Hiking
1. Do not travel alone. Do not hike after dark.
2. Make your presence known by making noise. Use caution where vision is obstructed.
3. Avoid bears when seen. Never approach or attempt to feed bears or other wildlife.
4. Avoid carcasses; bears often defend this source of food.

When Camping
1. Do not camp in areas frequented by bears.
2. Do not carry or use odorous foods.
3. Use "pack-in, pack-out" policy. Carry out all trash.
4. Regulations require that, when not in use, all odorous items including food, cooking gear, toiletries, and garbage be suspended at least 10 feet above the ground and 4 feet out from the trunk of the tree.
5. Sleep at least 100 yards or more from your food storage and cooking area.

When Fishing
Dispose of entrails by puncturing the air bladder and throwing into deep water, at least 100 yards from the nearest campsite or trail.

If You Encounter a Bear
1. Stay calm. Do not run. Many charges are bluff charges.
2. Slowly detour or back away.
3. If the bear attacks, play dead. Drop to the ground, lift your legs up to your chest, and clasp your hands over the back of your neck. Wearing your pack will shield your body.

Important: Information on bears is necessary to protect park visitors and bears. Report all bear sightings, bear sign, damage, or personal injuries to a park ranger.

There is no guarantee of your safety while hiking or camping in bear country.

---National Park Service---

Entering Bear Country—A Risk

(Courtesy Yellowstone National Park)

6

Recommended Reading

This list of recommended references will enhance your knowledge about bears, their habitat, and their behavior; teach you how to identify their sign; and provide great reading about bears in general. The specific information in some of these sources, such as that on recognizing bear sign, is essential for you to be well prepared for backpacking in bear country. All of these books would be wonderful to have in your personal library, but if that is not possible, check your local libraries or with friends. The books marked (*) are essential reading.

Animal Tracks and Signs of North America, Richard P. Smith, Stackpole, 1982.

Bear Attacks, Stephen Herrero, Lyons & Burford, 1985.

Bear in Their World, Erwin Bauer, Outdoor Life Books, 1985.

Bears of the World, Terry Domico and Mark Newman, Facts on File, 1988.

Bears of Yellowstone, The, Paul Schullery, Roberts Rinehart, Inc., 1986.

Beast that Walks Like Man, The, Harold McCracken, The Garden City Press, 1955.

Black Bear, Daniel J. Cox, Chronicle Books, 1990.

Black Bear: The Spirit of Wilderness, Barbara Ford, Houghton Mifflin, 1981.

Field Guide to Animal Tracks, A, Olaus J. Murie, Houghton, Mifflin, 1954.

Field Guide to Mammal Tracking in Western America, A, James Halfpenny, Johnson Publishing Co., 1986.

Great Bear Almanac, The, Gary Brown, Lyons & Burford, 1993.

Grizzly Bear, The, Thomas McNamee, Alfred A. Knopf, 1984.

Guide to Animal Tracking and Behavior, A (A Stokes Nature Guide), Donald and Lilian Stokes, Little, 1986.

Killer Bears, Mike Cramond, Charles Scribner's Sons, 1981.

No Room for Bears, Frank Dufresne, Holt, Rinehart and Winston, Inc., 1965.

Sacred Paw, The, Paul Shepard and Barry Sanders, Viking, Penguin, Inc., 1985.

Wild Bears, The, George Laycock, Outdoor Life Books, 1986.

Tracking and the Art of Seeing (How To Read Animal Tracks and Sign), Paul Rezendes, Camden House Publishers, 1992.

White Bear, Charles T. Feazel, Henry Holt Co., 1990.

INDEX

alertness, hiking and, 97–98
attacks, 4, 33–34, 40–44,
    103–104, 131–133
  causes of, 35–40
attitude, 47
audiovisual programs, 49

backcountry travel, 64–67
backpacks, storage of, 66*illus.*
bear behavior
  climbing, 17
  day beds, 18, 60, 94
  feeding, 14–15
  hibernation, 19–21
  play, 17
  reproduction, 18–19
  swimming, 16*illus.*, 16–17,
    107, 108, 130
  travel, 15–16
"bear country," 12, 46–47
  arrival in, 70–71
  knowledge about, 47–50
  transportation in, 61–67
  traveling in, 72–89, 92–102
  women in, 118–119
bear repellents, 134–136,
    135*illus.*
bear-resistant storage facilities,
    86
bears, 7–11
  attacks by, 4, 33–44,
    103–104, 131–133
  attractants, 51–56
  behavior, 14–21
  body language of, 121–131
  books about, 141–143
  communication between, 23
  differences between black
    and grizzly bears, 24, 25*map*,
    26–31
  encounters with, 4, 24,

  33–35, 121–122
  habitat, 12–13
  intelligence of, 22–23, 140
  observing and
    photographing, 102–104
  sense of smell, 11, 51, 99
bear sign, recognizing, 56–61,
    57–58*illus.*, 61*illus.*, 69–70,
    100
bear trails, 60
bicycling, 104–105
binoculars, 100, 102, 116
black bears, 7, 8*illus.*, 26*illus.*
  claws, 10*illus.*
  danger of, 121
  distribution, 24, 25*map*, 26
  foods, 31
  habitat, 30
  physical attributes, 26–29
  scat, 58
  tracks, 30*illus.*
bluff charges, 130
breaking camp, 94–95
brown bears, 7
bulletin boards and signs, 71,
    74, 76–77*illus.*, 92, 142*illus.*

caches, 59–60
camp equipment, 54–55
campgrounds, 74–75, 78*illus.*,
    80*illus.*, 81*illus.*
  cooking, 81–83
  food storage and, 84–88
  sanitation, 88–89, 92–93
  selecting a site, 75–79
  sleeping arrangements, 79–80
  at trailheads, 96
  water travel and, 107–108
  in winter, 111–112
Campho-Phenique, as bear
    attractant, 55

Canada, bears in, 25*map*, 26
capsaicin, 136
carrion, 59, 75, 77, 113
clothing, 54–55, 114–115
cooking equipment, 53–54
cooking odors, 114
critical space, invasion of,
    37–39, 38*illus.*, 69, 117
cubs, 20, 21, 22, 39*illus.*,
    39–40, 41, 125–126, 126*illus.*

day beds, 18, 60, 94
dens, 19–20
diurnal activity, 21
dogs, 110, 116
dominance, 22, 23

emergency planning, 68
encounters, 4, 24, 33–35,
    121–122
  avoiding, 45–70
  bear aware of you, 123–125
  bear not aware of you,
    122–123
  with bold black bears,
    126–127
  caused by dogs, 110
  confrontational situations,
    127–131
  reporting, 137
  sows with cubs, 125–126,
    126*illus.*
  while fishing, 113–114
  while hunting, 115–117
  while jogging, 117–118
experienced travelers, learning
    from, 49
eye contact with a bear, 129,
    130

feeding bears, 70, 84
field guides, 48
fighting a bear, 133
fires, 112, 119

fish and game departments,
    48–49
fishing, 108–109, 113–115
fish remnants, as bear sign, 60,
    77, 114
food attractants, 52–53, 70,
    82–83
food conditioning, 36, 74, 79,
    83, 114
food storage, 83–88
  hanging method, 65–67,
    66*illus.*, 90–91*illus.*
  water travel and, 108
  in winter, 112

garbage, as bear food, 34, 35,
    36, 53*illus.*, 54, 70, 88, 92
grizzly bears, 2–3, 7, 9*illus.*,
    16*illus.*, 27*illus.*, 33*illus.*,
    38–39*illus.*, 53*illus.*
  claws, 10*illus.*
  danger of, 121
  distribution, 24, 25*map*, 26
  foods, 31
  habitat, 30–31
  physical attributes, 26–30
  scat, 58, 58*illus.*
  tracks, 30*illus.*, 57*illus.*
guided hikes, 50, 71
"gut piles," 116–117

habituation, 36
hanging attractants, 87,
    90–91*illus.*, 105, 112, 117
Herrero, Stephen, 45
hibernation, 13, 19–21, 111
hierarchy, 22, 23
hiking, 94, 97–102
home ranges, 13
horses, traveling with,
    109–110
hunting, 115–117
hyperphagia, 19

injuries, 137

jogging, 117–118

land management agencies, 48
latrine areas, 92
lodging areas, 73
  cooking in, 81
  food storage in, 83–84
  sanitation, 88

marking, 23
menstrual odors, 118–119
motorcycling, 105–106

nocturnal activity, 21
noise, alerting bears with, 65,
  93, 99, 105

personal cleanliness, 55, 93
physical condition, hikers and,
  67–68
picnic areas, 72–73
playing dead, 42–43, 131–132
polar bears, 7
population density, 13
property, security of, 96–97
protection of young, 39–40
provoked encounters, 34

ranger stations, 68, 71
roadside areas, 72–73
running from a bear, 9–10,
  43–44, 128
R.V. and trailer camping, 81,
  84–85

safety, principles of, 68–70
scat, 23, 58, 77
scented toiletries, 55–56, 84,
  119
sexual activity (human), 55, 93

shuttles, 96
side trips, hiking and, 101–102
signing, 23
sows (adult females), 20, 21,
  22, 39*illus.*, 39–40, 41,
  125–126, 126*illus.*
stripped bark, as bear sign, 60,
  61*illus.*
surprising a bear, 37, 42–43,
  69, 98–99

tracks, 30*illus.*, 56–58, 57*illus.*,
  77
trail closures, 71, 72*illus.*
trailheads, 95–97
trail stops, 100–101
travel groups, 50, 64–65, 98
tree climbing to escape a bear,
  133–134

United States, bears in, 25*map*,
  26
unprovoked encounters, 35
urination, 23
Ursus americanus. See black
  bears
Ursus arctos horribilis. See
  grizzly bears

vehicles, 62–64, 83–84
  parking and food security, 95
videotapes, 49

wastewater, 54, 89, 92
water travel, 106–109
wildlife management agencies,
  71
winter travel, 111–112
women, precautions for,
  118–119

zoos/wildlife parks, 50